The Japanese Family System in Transition

LTCB International Library Selection No. 6

THE JAPANESE FAMILY SYSTEM IN TRANSITION

A Sociological Analysis of Family Change in Postwar Japan

OCHIAI EMIKO

Associate Professor
International Research Center for
Japanese Studies

LTCB International Library Foundation

Transcription of names

The Hepburn system of romanization is used for Japanese terms, including the names of persons and places. Long vowels are not indicated. With regard to personal names, the local custom of placing the family name first has been followed.

This book was originally published in 1994 by
Yuhikaku Publishing Co., Ltd. under the title
Nijuisseiki kazoku e: Kazoku no sengo taisei no mikata, koekata.
© 1994 by Ochiai Emiko

English translation rights arranged with Yuhikaku Publishing Co., Ltd.
© 1996 by LTCB International Library Foundation

First English edition published October 1997
by LTCB International Library Foundation
1-8, Uchisaiwaicho 2-chome, Chiyoda-ku; Tokyo 100, Japan
Tel: 03-5223-7204   Fax: 03-5511-8123

Translation and production by The Simul Press, Inc., Tokyo

Printed in Japan
ISBN 4-924971-06-5 C1336 ¥3000E

CONTENTS

Chapter 7

"NEW FAMILY" MEETS THE HOUSEWIFE'S MALAISE

Chapter 8

ARE TODAY'S PARENTS BAD PARENTS?

Chapter 9

BILATERALITY AND THE FUTURE OF THE *IE*

Chapter 10

TOWARD A SOCIETY WITH THE INDIVIDUAL AS UNIT

The LTCB International Library Foundation Statement of Purpose

Introduction to the English Edition

What image does "a Japanese family" convey? A patriarchal, autocratic husband and a quiet, attentive wife? Studious children burdened with after-school tutoring, and a mother who pressures them to succeed in entrance exams? Or a multi-generational household whose elderly members are valued and respected? For some readers, perhaps no image will come to mind. For many years, the image of Japan introduced overseas consisted of "culture" in the narrow sense—Japanese gardens, Zen, the tea ceremony. In the last twenty years, there has been growing interest in the Japanese economy and Japanese-style management, but relatively little information has been available on many other facets of Japanese society and daily life. This volume on the postwar Japanese family has been included in the LTCB International Library of Japan in the hope of righting the balance to some extent, and I am delighted that my book has been granted this valuable opportunity to reach an audience outside Japan.

There is one thing which I trust readers of the English edition will keep in mind: this volume is not an introduction to established theories or the conventional wisdom within Japan. On the contrary, it was written in an attempt to overturn the self-concept of postwar Japanese society, and many Japanese readers have told me that they did indeed find it "eye-opening."

What was the conventional wisdom about postwar Japan that I was attempting to overturn? It would be no exaggeration to say that the self-concept of postwar Japan, or, more broadly, modern Japan, has been shaped by constant contrast with the West. Orientalism is hardly restricted to the Occident. In the Orient—

the object of Orientalist discourse—the phenomenon has occurred in inverted form. An East-versus-West dichotomy has been adopted as a conceptual framework, and characteristics regarded as Oriental have been made the core of identity. While value judgments toward this identity may have differed, ranging from pride in being Oriental to a desire to erase these characteristics, the dualistic framework remains.

This same phenomenon has also occurred with regard to family theory in postwar Japan. The postwar Japanese family has been understood within the following basic framework: the Western family is typically a nuclear family consisting of husband, wife, and children, while the Japanese family was originally a unique social system, the *ie* (discussed in chapter 4), produced by a unique culture, and the *ie* has been transformed into the nuclear family through the process of social change known as modernization.

The key concept of the analysis in this book, however, is the "modern family." This concept, developed by social historians of the family, was first applied in Europe, but I believe it is also useful in describing family change accompanying modernization in other regions of the world, and I hope that this volume will serve to demonstrate its usefulness. I have also emphasized changes in demographic conditions as important explanatory factors of family change. Combining the concept of the modern family and the particular demographic conditions of postwar Japan, in this book I have proposed a new concept named the Postwar Family System.

Neither the birth of the modern family nor the demographic changes accompanying modernization are peculiar to a particular cultural area; both are found fairly universally in modern societies. In my view, the unique form taken by the family in each society in the modern era is the result of subtle interactions among a number of factors, including differences in the speed of universal changes and the effects of the existing cultural substrate. Rather than viewing the West as the universal type and Japan as special, I prefer to think that both are variations which have occurred on common ground.

This volume departs from the conventional wisdom in other ways besides its view of Japan and the West. By taking the approach of modern family theory, it also challenges the conventional idea of what a family is. A recurrent theme of this book, based on the findings of family historians, is that the family we have long taken for granted—a father who works to support the household, a mother who is a full-time housewife, and two or three treasured children—is not historically immutable, but is merely one form which became established at a particular point in time, that is, the modern era. I am very interested to know whether this revised view of the family is already accepted as common knowledge among readers of the English edition, but in Japan, at least, this relativized view of the modern family has only recently begun to gain the attention of the general public.

One further feature of this volume is a chapter which analyzes the thinking of the Japanese women's movement of the early 1970s while quoting the movement's pamphlets and other writings—a feature which is unusual even in Japan. I am often asked by friends abroad "Is there a women's movement in Japan?" Of course there was and still is, even if it has become somewhat low-key. Although the Japanese women's movement drew strength from its European and American counterparts as it got under way in the 1970s, rather than importing the ideas of the West, to a great extent the movement developed its own ideas and expressed them in its own way, and I have tried here to reconstruct their thinking from their own words.

I would like to take this opportunity to thank the many people who have made the publication of this English edition possible. I would like to express my gratitude to Uehara Takeshi, Miyado Yoshio, and Shinkai Hisayuki of the LTCB International Library Foundation, who first proposed the translation project, to the many staff members at Simul International, Inc., for their patient and efficient teamwork during the long process of translating, revising, and producing the English text, and especially to Geraldine Harcourt, who brought to the translation not only her careful attention to accuracy but also her background knowledge of the women's movement in Japan. I also wish to thank the editor of the Japanese-language edition, Mitsuda Yasuko of Yuhikaku Publishing Co., Ltd., for her generous help in the preparation of this version; Kurioka Namie, for the attractive cover illustration; Unno Kayoko, for her help in preparing the original manuscript; and Yatabe Hiromi, for her assistance in updating the tables and figures. Last, but not least, I would like to extend my appreciation to Professors Arichi Toru and Haga Toru, for their support and encouragement in the publication of both the Japanese and the English editions.

Prologue

THE POSTWAR PERIOD TAKES A CURTAIN CALL

In the spring of 1990 I spent day after day in the Oya Soichi Library in Tokyo, thumbing through its vast collection of old magazines and studying how the visual representation of women has changed over time. In the course of this research, as I looked at the miniskirted figures of yesteryear and the grandes dames of the screen in their ingenue days, I was struck by an intriguing observation: there seem to be fashions, or eras, in the way that women smile.

In images from the first few years after Japan's defeat in World War II, women had regained the ability to smile, but they did so bashfully, their heads slightly bowed. By 1950, however, they were all looking up, turning their faces to the sky with enormous grins. Then the angle of the head was steadily lowered while the expression gradually stiffened, year by year, until by 1955 the women's gaze was approximately level and their lips wore a very artificial smile. This was not a matter of two or three similar pictures appearing by chance at the same time. In magazines of every type, whether in illustrators' drawings or glossy photos of movie stars, all the women in any given period wore expressions that were uncannily alike.

What is even more curious is that after 1955 the smiles remained essentially unchanged until the mid-1970s. Although there was a temporary break with the past around 1970, influenced by the "sexual revolution" taking place throughout the industrial world, by 1975 the same expression was nearly univer-

1

sal again. (The departure was greatest in magazines for single women, and the return most complete in magazines for house-wives.) Then, in the latter half of the 1970s, there began an era of image experimentation which brought changes as rapid as those that had preceded the previous two decades of stability.[1]

This small discovery gave me the germ of the idea for this book, which can best be summarized as follows: Although the postwar period in Japan has often been characterized as an era of rapid change, in my view it would be more accurate to describe it in terms of a certain period during which the society maintained a stable structure, or what might be called a particular social system, preceded by a distinct phase during which this structure emerged, and followed by another distinct phase during which it underwent change.

This view seems to be borne out by more casual, day-to-day observations. The fact that "retro" revivals of the styles of the past have come to a stop with the early 70s is one such indication. The music and fashions of several eras have recently enjoyed "retro" booms, and have been featured in many TV commercials and car-toons, for instance. But not every era has had its turn in the limelight. First there was a fascination with the *fin de siècle*, fol-lowed by the 1920s and 1930s, in each case featuring images mainly from European and American culture. Japanese images were at the heart of revivals of the 50s and 60s, but the "retro" phenomenon seems unlikely to extend to the years immediately after the Second World War,[2] nor to the two decades of the more recent past.

Old things or ideas do not inspire nostalgia simply by being old. People become nostalgic when something evokes their own experience, when it is somehow connected to their present lives. Yet if this thing or idea happens still to exist today in essentially the same form, it becomes merely old and boring. It is when we recognize some part of our own personal origins on the verge of being lost that we feel the emotion we call nostalgia.

In this sense, the era known in Japan as the postwar period is currently in the limelight. Like a performer after the final curtain, it has been called onstage by the audience's applause for one last bow. Perhaps it is this widely shared sense of nostalgia which has prompted me to look back at the postwar years at this particular moment. For this moment offers a perspective from which it seems possible, at least in regard to the family, to review the postwar period as a completed era with a structure of its own.

BEYOND THEORIES OF THE FAMILY IN CRISIS

My motive for writing this book was not solely to reflect upon times gone by, however. I was also prompted by the need to answer questions which look to the future.

The need to find answers as to where the family is heading and what it will be like in the twenty-first century is felt widely and with increasing urgency in Japan. The perception that the family is undergoing rapid change extends throughout society, from the government, the media, and academic circles to the general public. Today, such topics as the falling birthrate have become part of everyday conversation, frequently coming up even in speeches at weddings. Many people apparently see these changes as a vaguely defined "crisis of the family." For example, when I ask a college class or general audience "Who thinks that the family these days is in trouble?" well over half raise their hands. But how valid are the grounds for this impression?

One series of data which has fueled the sense of crisis in the media and among the public is the "New Social Indicators" (later renamed "People's Life Indicators"), released annually since the mid-1970s by the Social Policy Bureau of the Economic Planning Agency. The Bureau's statisticians have divided the quality of life in Japan into eight broad areas. As indicators they use quantitative measures of economic stability, environmental quality, safety, health, quality of working life, etc., designating each item either positive or negative; the positive and negative values are then integrated in each area to assess its overall quality. According to the Bureau's figures, while every other area has steadily improved since 1975, "family life" alone has shown a marked deterioration. The decline was particularly serious from the late 1970s through 1983. On receiving the Bureau's annual press releases during these years, every newspaper gave prominent coverage to the supposed crisis of the family.

When we examine the actual indices more closely, however, we notice something odd. Negative factors which contributed significantly to the decline in the index of family life included the rate of juvenile delinquency as well as the rate of extended absenteeism among elementary and junior high school pupils—neither of which can be said solely to reflect the state of the family. Another negative factor was the number of elderly people living alone; however, a rise in this number is unavoidable to some extent, simply for demographic reasons, and besides, there are probably some older people who prefer to live by themselves. Furthermore, because the Social Policy Bureau also used the latter statistic as an index in international comparisons, it gave family life a low rating in Western countries where it is customary for adult daughters and sons to live apart from their parents, and thus fostered the misguided but widely accepted notion that while the Japanese family was in crisis, it was still in much better shape than families in the West. (These problems were largely eliminated in 1992, in a major revision of the People's Life Indicators for which I served on the advisory committee.)

A vague sense that the family is in crisis has, in fact, existed throughout the postwar period, more as a kind of unconscious mood than as a conclusion based on solid data. In the late 1950s and early 1960s, government publications such as the *White Paper on Health and Welfare* discussed the war's legacy of social problems, which included large numbers of orphans and single-mother households, and at the same time cited as a problem the weakness of the postwar family resulting from the abolition of the legal framework of the *ie* system, Japan's traditional family system which placed great importance on the continuity of the family line. And it seems that this concern was not limited to the government. While people welcomed liberation from the *ie* where husband-wife relationships were concerned, they were not without misgivings when it came to changes affecting the relations of parents and children, as famously depicted by director Ozu Yasujiro's films such as *Tokyo Story*.

By the mid- to late 1960s, when the "nuclearization" of the family is said to have progressed at the height of Japan's rapid economic growth, overt calls for the restoration of the old family system were no longer heard. Instead, the tenor of debate now focused chiefly on the fragility of the nuclear family and the social strains produced by high growth. The form of commentary on the family which was in favor at this time was thus a fusion of what could be called a critique of capitalism and a critique of the vestiges of feudalism as embodied in the *ie* system.

In the 1970s, phrases like "the dissolution of the family" and "the breakdown of the family" became the standard vocabulary when discussing family issues. It was no longer one special type of family, such as the *ie*, that was believed to be in crisis; rather, it was the family in the broadest possible sense. It was also during the latter half of the 1970s that the government adopted "strengthening the foundations of the home" as a policy goal, while its social indicators warned of the deterioration of family life from year to year. In 1983, family problems were the subject of a special edition of the *White Paper on the National Life* (informally known as the "White Paper on the Family").

An investigation into why the crisis of the family was heralded so insistently throughout the postwar period would no doubt make a very interesting study in the history of consciousness. But to anyone concerned with the history of the family itself, this situation is far from helpful when one is trying to pin down evidence and build a solid argument. A feeling that the family is sinking fast has persisted in one form or another, from the dissolution of the *ie* to the "breakdown of the family," and yet the various theories that have been put forward flatly contradict one another as to possible causes. It seems to me that there has been surprisingly little debate about which theories come nearest the truth, or, at an even more fundamental level, how we can distinguish pathological from normal change, and whether the family was ever actually in crisis.

If we are truly to find clues to guide us out of crisis—or the myth of crisis—I believe it is essential that we first distance ourselves clearly from the phenomena and take another look. This process will include reconsidering the grounds for determining whether or not a crisis or pathology exists. What is required here is not an inflammatory discourse of crisis but a coolheaded analysis of change. And the starting point is a reexamination of the recent past. This is not as circuitous an approach as it may appear: in order to find out where we are heading, we must know exactly where we have been. In other words, to gain insight into the family in the twenty-first century, we must first be clear about its nature in the twentieth century.

THE ORGANIZATION OF THIS BOOK

Thus, what I am actually setting out to discuss under the original title of this book, "Toward the Twenty-First-Century Family," is a sociological analysis of family change in postwar Japan. I intend to go beyond a historical review of postwar changes, however, and attempt to construct a sound theoretical basis for projecting an understanding of the past into the future.

The chapters that follow are in broadly chronological order. At the same time, they are organized to present a concept which I have tentatively named the "Postwar Family System." By this I mean the nature of the family during that period after the war in which, as I suggested earlier, family structure remained relatively stable. In chapters 1 through 4 I will sketch the development of three characteristics which I attribute to the Postwar Family System, namely, the housewifization of women, reproductive egalitarianism, and the effects of demographic transition, and in chapter 5 I will provide an overview of the ideas discussed up to that point. Chapters 6 through 9 will deal with the period in which, after its completion, the Postwar Family System began to undergo change. In these chapters I will explore a number of problems which arose in the family during this transition and which have been viewed as symptoms of crisis, and I will attempt to reframe these problems in relation to the three characteristics. Finally, in chapter 10, I will predict, as far as possible, the future direction of the Japanese family.

The concept of the modern family, developed through studies of the social history of the family, will be pivotal to this discussion.

I will also draw extensively on the theories of historical demography, which forms the basis of social history as a discipline. Also, at many points in these pages, I expect readers will become aware of a distinctly female viewpoint, fostered by the field of women's studies. While this book was certainly not written for women only, in light of my experience teaching at a women's university I have tried to ensure that it serves, in part, as a kind of message to my younger sisters. That is, I hope that women, and of course men, will find this book helpful in thinking about their own family.

The concept of this book took shape gradually in the course of discussions with many people in a variety of places, including classrooms and auditoriums. There have even been some people who have consulted me for personal advice. The feedback I have received in all these exchanges has been invaluable, and in the hope of re-creating some sense of these live interactions I have decided to write in a conversational rather than an academic style. My aim is not to deliver explanations in cut-and-dried textbook fashion but to challenge the generally accepted way of looking at the family and propose a different one. I invite readers to approach this book as if listening to a lecture series presented live, with each chapter being a separate lecture devoted to one topic.

Chapter 1 | Have Women Always Been Housewives?

A NEIGHBORLY CHAT

Until recently I lived in a condominium, which is known in Japan as a *manshon* (mansion). An interesting thing about *manshon* complexes is that because all the owners have bought at a similar price they tend to be in the same age group, and where I lived was no exception. This meant that our children were also much the same age, a fact which naturally led to many neighborly contacts and conversations.

Several years ago, I was chatting one day with a woman who lived in my complex when she suddenly blurted out: "You know, I don't think I'm cut out to be a housewife. I don't really seem to like housework very much. Or looking after children, either. We've got one child, but I don't want to have another."

As this was a woman with a reputation as an expert home-maker, the kind that everyone in the *manshon* complex turned to for advice, I was astonished to hear her talk like this. But what she really meant, I suspect, was "I'm not suited to doing *nothing but* housework."

Because she was a perfectionist she carried out her duties per-fectly, and yet it seems that in her heart she felt more alive when she was an "OL" ("office lady"). Knowing her, I'm sure she was very good at her office job, a real go-getter. But she believed that a woman was supposed to marry and, once married, have chil-dren, and that this meant staying at home full-time—and that was what she did. Eventually, though, she began to have second thoughts.

"Why is it," she asked intensely, "that women have always been housewives? Can you tell me why men work outside the home and women are housewives?" At that moment, the proverbial penny dropped: for the first time, I understood clearly why I was doing the kind of research that I do.

When people asked the subject of my work, I used to give various replies: the sociology of the family, or the history of women, or social history. This did not always satisfy them, and I often ended up giving a longwinded explanation. But suddenly I realized that, in a nutshell, what I had been trying to do in my research was to answer that very question: "Why are women housewives?"

Practically every woman alive in most countries today must have pondered this question at one time or another, even if she has never discussed it with others. Whether she frames it negatively ("Who says I have to be a housewife?") or positively, whether she rebels or conforms, the expectation that women become housewives must always form a reference point in a woman's thinking about her life choices.

I too pondered this question at one point in my own life, and became involved in my present line of research while pursuing the answer. At first I was under the impression that in order to solve a problem of such magnitude I would have to retrace human history to somewhere around the point where Homo sapiens evolved from the apes. In the end, though, I discovered that the answer lay just around the corner.

THE M-SHAPED CURVES OF FIVE GENERATIONS

Before attempting to answer the question of why women become housewives, we need to examine the underlying assumption that they have always done so. Even among the audiences I speak to in Japan, surprisingly few people are aware of the statistical trends I am about to describe.

The curves in figure 1-1 show the labor force participation rate, by age, of women in eight countries. To obtain these curves, we take the total number of women in each age group, find the percentage who work, and plot these values for all age groups.

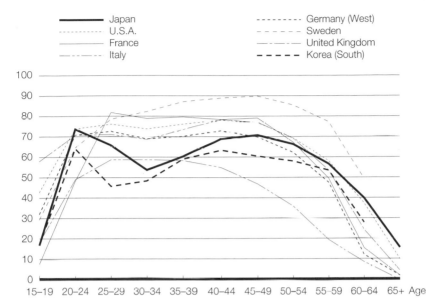

Fig. 1-1. Age-specific female labor force participation rates in selected countries

Note: Figures are for 1995 in Japan, 1993 in the U.K., and 1994 in all other countries.
Sources: For Japan: Statistics Bureau, Management and Coordination Agency, *Rodoryoku chosa* (Labor force survey); for all other countries: ILO, *Yearbook of Labour Statistics, 1994.*

The resulting curves for Japan and South Korea are known as "M-shaped curves," since the pattern of two peaks with a trough between them resembles the letter M. Britain also had the same type of curve until quite recently. This pattern reflects the fact that many women work while they are single, leave their jobs on marrying or starting a family, and return to the workforce when their children are more independent. M-shaped curves are very typical patterns of female labor force participation, but they are not universal. The United States and Sweden currently provide the best examples of what is known as the "reversed U-shaped curve," where the dip in the M has disappeared altogether and the top of the curve is a plateau, like that of male employment graphs.

The usual way of presenting information using an M-shaped curve is to plot a single line and call it the curve of women's labor force participation rate by age for a particular year. But this type of graph does not map individual women's real lives. For example, a twenty-year-old looking at the current curve may want to check what is happening in the older age groups, one by one, to see what the graph tells her about her own future. She may trace its ups and downs and think, "So the chances are that I'll quit my job around 30, and be working again by 40 with a probability of x percent, and when I'm 50. . . ." In reality, however, there is no one whose life fits a single curve. An individual who was 20 years old in 1990 will reappear among the 30-year-olds in the graph for 2000, and among the 40-year-olds in the graph for 2010. So the 20-year-old looking at the curve for 1990 is not seeing a prediction of her future. If she looks at the age group to which her mother current-ly belongs, she sees what her mother's generation is doing now, but their behavior provides no clues to what she herself will be doing at the same age.

To approximate the reality of women's lives, we need a sepa-rate curve of labor force participation by age for each cohort, or (in everyday language) each generation. This is the case in figure 1-2, with curves for Japanese women born in 1926–30, 1936–40, 1946–50, 1956–60, and 1966–70.

I have shown this graph to Japanese audiences of various ages, especially when there are women present, and invited them to guess which curve belongs to which age group. Not many guess right. Note that Group C has the M-shaped curve which dips deepest; this is in fact the age group born in 1946–50. Group B, with the next deepest trough, were born in 1936–40. Group A, born in 1926–30, have maintained a relatively smooth curve at a relatively high level throughout their collective lifetime. The trough of their M-shaped curve, though not shown here, is shal-lower than Group B's and similar to that of Group D, who were born in 1956–60, while Group E, born in 1966–70, are on the shallowest path. It is interesting that even when there are large numbers of people representing each generation in an audience, few can accurately identify these curves. Clearly there are some patterns of which we remain unaware, even as we are living them.

THE POSTWAR TURN TOWARD THE HOME

The significant part of figure 1-2 is the trough of the M. It is quite shallow in the group of women born in 1926–30. Then, in the two groups that follow, it rapidly becomes deeper. What are we to make of this? Having heard it said often enough that women's participation in Japanese society has increased since the war, we are apt to associate postwar change in this area with a gradual decline in the proportion of full-time housewives and an increase in the proportion of working women. Further, we tend to assume that this trend has recently accelerated. However, this is not the case.

The right-hand peak of the M, the peak of reentry to the labor force after raising a family, may indeed be on the rise. But it is what happens at the bottom of the curve that is critical. As a result of Japanese employment practices, once a woman has left the workplace and devoted herself full-time to the home, when she returns to work it will most likely be as a part-timer, with status and pay clearly inferior to those of full-time staff. Essentially, housewives with part-time jobs are still housewives. Society

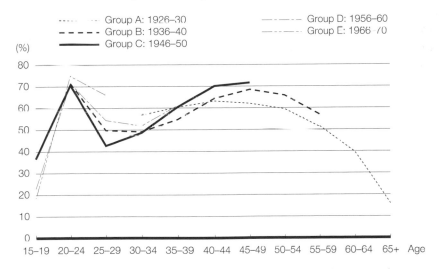

Fig. 1-2. Age-specific female labor force participation rates in Japan by birth cohort

Source: Statistics Bureau, Management and Coordination Agency, *Rodoryoku chosa* (Labor force survey).

regards them as such, and they are inclined to think of themselves in the same way. One often hears words to the effect that "I'm a housewife, so naturally I take time off from work to attend to family matters."

Thus, whether she stays home at the time of marriage, childbirth, and child rearing is a decisive factor in shaping a woman's identity. The trough of the M, which represents staying at home, rapidly became deeper in the three groups born in 1926–30, 1936–40, and 1946–50. Although this sounds like the reverse of what we are used to hearing, we need to recognize the fact clearly: Women did not begin to participate in the workforce after the war; rather, they began to stay at home. After the war, women became increasingly oriented toward the role of housewife.

Note, however, that after the M-shaped curves had deepened for two decades, the trend reversed. The bottom of the M for those born in 1956–60 is shallower than it was for those born in 1936–40 and 1946–50. And while it took two decades to drop, since then, in the same length of time, the bottom of the M has not only rebounded but is headed toward an all-time high, as shown by the slope of the curve for those born in 1966–70. If an ongoing trend showed this kind of acceleration it would not be particularly unusual, but here we are seeing a remarkable about-face: a complete reversal of the trend toward the home.

The Japanese media have given extensive coverage to the ways in which women's lives have changed over the past two decades, but they have tended to portray these changes as fashionable, superficial phenomena of pop culture. Figure 1-2 makes it clear that the changes were no mere fad or mood of the moment; rather, they were pivotal events having genuine substance.

What this means is that young women today cannot live as their mothers did. This is not a question of values. They may think their mothers' way of life was good, or perhaps easy or secure, but the social conditions that would allow them to imitate their mothers' lives no longer exist. Anyone who tried to live the same way today would have to swim deliberately, and strongly, against the current.

Until now we have been looking at the age- and cohort-specific profiles of women's labor force participation rates. We would find a similar story if we took the overall female labor force participation rate, which is simply the proportion of women who work to the total female population aged 15 or over. According to the labor force statistics published by the Statistics Bureau of the Management and Coordination Agency, this ratio followed a downward path for three decades after the war. In 1955 it stood at 56.7 percent, falling to 54.5 percent in 1960, 50.6 percent in 1965, and 45.7 percent in 1975. The downward trend resulted from a combination of two factors: a longer period of education in the youngest age group, and the deepening trough of the M in the childbearing and child-rearing years. Together, the resulting decreases more than offset the increase in women returning to work after rearing a family. But the female labor force participation rate bottomed out in 1975,[1] and by 1990 had risen to 50.1 percent—further illustrating the point that postwar change has not been uniformly in one direction.

THE ERA OF HIGH GROWTH AND THE SHIFT TO FULL-TIME HOMEMAKING

Thus, although one might have assumed that Japanese women were more housebound the further back in time one goes, it turns out that a surprisingly high proportion of women born in the late 1920s have worked all their lives, while those born in the late 1940s stayed home in greater numbers.

People born between 1947 and 1949 comprise the *dankai no sedai* ("clumped generation")—Japan's baby boomers, the generation synonymous with the campus rebellion of 1968–69. The women of this age group were young at the time of *uman ribu* ("women's lib"; a phase of the Japanese women's movement in the early 1970s). The fact that this same generation produced the highest proportion of full-time homemakers in Japanese women's history seems to belie the active, assertive image we have of them as young women. This puzzle, however, can be readily explained by the fact that the nation's industrial structure was changing.

With the structural transformation of the economy that took place during the era of rapid growth from the late 1950s to 1973, the base of Japan's social structure shifted from the farmer and the small business operator to the white-collar company employee or "salaryman." Women born in the 1920s had typically married into a household which either farmed or owned a small shop or factory, where they worked alongside other members of the extended family. But since salarymen's wives generally became full-time housewives, during the high-growth era the increase in families headed by white-collar workers was accompanied by a shift for women toward full-time domestic duties.

I live on the outskirts of Kyoto, in a part of the city where there are rice paddies and vegetable gardens just beyond the housing developments. When my daughter was a baby I often strolled her to the park along a road that ran between fields. It was not as if I was short of things to do, but no matter how busy or tired I was, I knew I had to make sure the baby got enough sun and fresh air. If I neglected our daily walk, I told myself, she would cry at night and have all sorts of problems.

Once, seeing me pushing the baby carriage, one of the older farm women whom I had gotten to know observed, "You young folk these days are lucky. All you've got to do is play."

So much for my conscientious parenting. To my farmer friend, bringing up children was something you did in your spare time. She never had the option of committing all her time to it. Women who have spent their lives working in the fields say, "I used to nurse the baby sitting on the ridge between the rice paddies, and that was the only time I got to rest." I thought breast-feeding was hard work. It left me feeling worn out and sleepy, as if the baby had sucked up all my strength. But the other duties of young wives in the old farm households must have been so demanding that, for them, breast-feeding was a break.

But while noting that women of older generations worked at the family trade throughout their lives, we should also bear in mind that such work differs in important ways from employment. The most obvious difference is the absence of a salary. The income from the business is paid to the head of the household, and no matter how hard they may work, the women do not receive a share which is theirs to spend as they wish. The other major difference is that in a family farm or small business, the workplace is in or adjacent to the home.

Today, when a housewife works, she almost always seeks outside employment. Thus, the greatest change in the structure of female labor is the fact that when women work now, they do so outside the home and earn wages which are at their disposal. Accordingly, if we focus solely on employment rates, our impression that women's social participation has increased since the war is not entirely wrong. What *would* be entirely wrong is to assume that women in the past did not work, if this is defined as engaging in productive labor. Women have not always been full-time housewives. Although female labor in the past had a different structure, we should not allow this to obscure the fact that Japanese women have always worked at other jobs in addition to their household duties.

WHAT INTERNATIONAL COMPARISONS REVEAL

Finally, let us take a brief look at women's work from an international perspective. Today, we have the general impression that more women work outside the home in the West than in Japan, and I mentioned earlier that in the United States and Sweden, in particular, the labor force participation rate by age currently takes the form of a reversed U-shaped curve instead of an M-shaped curve. But has this always been the case?

Figure 1-3 shows long-term changes in the female labor force participation rate for various countries.[2] Around the turn of the century, Britain and the United States were among the countries that had a very low ratio of women (especially married women) in the labor force. By comparison, Japan was at the highest level, exceeding even those European countries, such as Germany, which had quite high ratios.

It is very difficult to extend this graph back to the nineteenth century, since accurate data on labor force participation rates are scarce, and even in those countries where censuses were conduct-

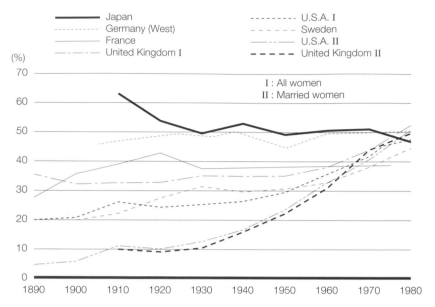

Fig. 1-3. Long-term trends of female labor force participation
rates, 1890–1980

Source: Mizuno Asao, ed., *Keizai sofutoka jidai no josei rodo* (Female labor in the age of the soft economy).[2]

ed, they tended to underreport female labor. With this proviso, Anita Nyberg has estimated female labor force participation rates in Sweden in the nineteenth and early twentieth centuries, and corrected for underreporting in the census. From her findings we gain a general picture of the curve's gradual descent over the last decades of the nineteenth century, until it reached the low level observed in the first half of the twentieth century.[3]

In premodern societies, the level of female labor force participation varies greatly according to the culture of the region. For example, cultural norms which require that women be secluded in the home or conceal their bodies from public view will tend to hold down their level of labor force participation. But women are known to have worked alongside men in agricultural societies in both Europe and Japan, tilling the fields and tending the animals. In such cultures we can plot, very schematically, a curve shaped like a V, as female labor force participation started at quite a high level, dipped, and then rose again.

As might be expected, there was a change in the content of this labor over time. Before the curve dipped, women had been engaged mainly in agricultural labor. This was partially replaced by factory labor even before the curve began to dip; later, as labor force participation began to rise again, it generally took the form of employment. What the dip represents is the shift to the housewife's role. Thus, with modernization, women's lives change in stages, not unidirectionally. It can be said, at least of Europe and Japan, that at a certain stage of the modernization process, women become full-time housewives and leave the workplace. After a period of variable duration in which women are housewives, they return to the workforce, this time as employed labor. Women in these countries have thus experienced a two-stage process of change in the course of modernization.[4]

In the case of Sweden, for example, this is directly observable as a fall followed by a rise in the female labor force participation rate. Japan, however, shows what I interpret as the typical pattern of latecomers in development, seen also to a certain extent in Germany. Latecomers modernize rapidly. Because of this, there is an overlap between the trend of housewifization, which lowers the female labor force participation rate, and the upward trend when women return to the workforce. The proportion of women in the labor force at any one time represents the sum of these two trends, and since the fall and the rise effectively cancel each other out, the curve remains more or less horizontal. This yields the pattern characteristic of latecomers in development, in which the V-shape caused by the sharp fall and subsequent rise of the labor force participation rate is not visible, even though, beneath the surface, the same types of change in the content of labor are going on. In latecomer countries, there is not time for all women to stay at home. While individual women do so to bear and rear children, there is strong demand for them to return to work as employed labor as soon as their children are grown. Thus, in the aggregate, there is no period when all women remain at home.

This phenomenon may be occurring at the present time in many societies. The Asian NIEs, or newly industrializing economies, such as South Korea, Taiwan, Hong Kong, and

Singapore, are currently pursuing a course of modernization along the same lines earlier taken by the Western nations and Japan. As seen in figure 1-4, a calculation of the female labor force participation rates by age for South Korea, the leading Asian NIE, reveals a pattern very similar to that of Japan. That is to say, the bottom of the M-shaped curves first dropped and then, in the 1970s, rebounded.[5]

In light of these trends, the decision of the Hong Kong-born TV personality Agnes Chan to take her infant child to work, which aroused controversy in Japan several years ago, could be seen as reflecting the rapidity of the changes in women's lives according to the pattern of latecomer nations, since Hong Kong is another rapid modernizer. In this pattern the female population as a whole continues working, with no generation staying permanently at home. Thus, younger women will naturally seek the advice of their mothers' generation with regard to their working lives. The older generation no doubt replies, "You want to know how to bring up a child while holding down a job? That's easy. Just take the child wherever you go and look after it while you work."

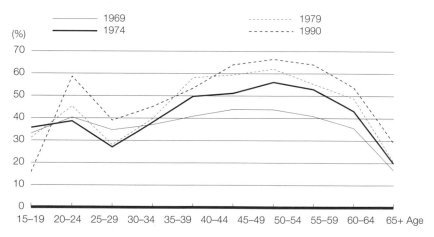

Fig. 1-4. Age-specific female labor force participation rates in South Korea, 1969-90

Source: National Statistical Office, Ministry of Finance and Economy, South Korea, *Statistic Yearbook of Korea*.

This historical background may also shed light on the reluctance of many mothers in Japan today to leave their children in day care. "If I could leave the children with my mother-in-law, or with my mother, I could go out to work," they often say, "but I don't like the idea of leaving them with strangers." When Japan was an agricultural society, the traditional practice was for women to leave the children with their mothers-in-law while they worked. Perhaps the psychological resistance to day care is rooted in this tradition.

We have come to take for granted the gender role that defines women as housewives, to the point where we assume that it is as ancient as Homo sapiens. But this assumption is wrong. The majority of women became full-time housewives only very recently—in Japan's case, during the era of rapid economic growth. The prevalence in our society of the norm expressed by such statements as "Women should be housewives" and "Women's primary role should be homemaking and child care" is no more ancient than that.

Chapter 2 | The Origins of Housework and the Housewife

WHAT IS A HOUSEWIFE?

In the previous chapter we found a rather unexpected answer to the question "Have women always been housewives?" We discovered that after World War II an increasing proportion of women became housewives, whereas it has usually been assumed that women's participation in postwar Japanese society had steadily increased. But perhaps chapter 1 relied a little too heavily on statistics. In this chapter, then, I would like to look at various aspects of the housewife and her historical origins.

The British sociologist Ann Oakley is the author of a number of books on this subject, including *The Sociology of Housework* and *Housewife*. She opens the latter by quoting two definitions of the term "housewife": "the person, other than a domestic servant, who is responsible for most of the household duties (or for supervising a domestic servant who carries out these duties)," or "a woman who manages or directs the affairs of her household; the mistress of a family; the wife of a householder."[1] Further, Oakley states that the characteristic features of the modern housewife role can be summarized as follows: (1) it is exclusively allocated to women; (2) it is economically dependent; (3) it is not accorded the status of work; (4) it is women's primary role.

A housewife, she says, is defined as a woman who does housework (though this may be called "household duties" or "the affairs of her household"). For this definition to be meaningful, then, we need to know what housework is.

I once tried asking students in my university classes this question. Among those who attempted a definition (instead of merely listing tasks such as cooking and doing laundry), a typical answer was "the work that enables a family to live comfortably."

In considering the question further, it may be useful to look at a series of controversies revolving around the housewife's role which surfaced in the Japanese media and have become known collectively as "the housewife debate." This debate developed in three phases: the first in 1955–59, the second in 1960–61, and the third in 1972. In light of our discussion of labor force participation rates in the previous chapter, we can see that the housewife debate coincided exactly with the high-growth era when Japanese women were flocking into the home.

The debate was started by an article entitled "The Secondary Occupation of Homemaking" by Ishigaki Ayako, which appeared in a leading women's magazine in 1955.[2] In this article, Ishigaki warned of the effects that staying home full-time had on women. "If a housewife endlessly repeats the same tasks from morning till night in the safety zone of the home," she writes, "her mental growth will be arrested." And "a housewife has become flabby in spirit . . . . Each day she lets precious hours of her life slip away." Though severely critical, the article seems to have been intended as a wake-up call to women, both those at home and those in paid employment.

Naturally, it provoked counterarguments. Some writers emphasized that the housewife's situation enabled her to become involved in social causes in a way that was impossible for men or other women with jobs outside the home, due to the restrictions on their time.[3] This has, in fact, proved to be the case: housewives today are a major force in many social movements, from consumers' cooperatives and environmental groups to election campaigns.

Another famous contribution to the debate was the "superfluous wife theory" of ethnographer Umesao Tadao, published in 1959.[4] Arguing that domestic labor would increasingly be mechanized or supplied through the market, he contended that "Married life in the future will gradually approach a state of cohabitation

between a man and woman who will have become socially homo-
geneous. It will no longer be a mutually complementary
relationship between the socially heterogeneous parties that we
know as 'husband' and 'wife.' Women will no longer need to be
wives, and men will no longer need to be husbands."

In essence, the first phase of the housewife debate raised all of
the points which remain controversial to this day, centered on the
issue of whether or not the housewife's role is important.

WHAT IS HOUSEWORK IN ECONOMIC TERMS?

The second phase (1960–61) focused on the nature of housework,
and became a debate about economics. A most unusual aspect of
this is that it preceded similar discussion in the West, where the
economics of domestic labor were hotly debated from the mid-
1970s, especially in Britain.[5] (It is a sad comment on the isolated
situation of the Japanese language that this discussion was not
sparked by the one in Japan but arose quite separately.)

In seeking to define housework in economic terms, writers at
this time asked whether it creates value. In other words, they
asked whether or not housework constitutes "labor." The underlying concept of labor was obviously that of Marxian economics,
which defines labor as human activity that creates value. "Value"
here means exchange value, or the ability to be sold—that is,
placed on the market and exchanged for money. Marxian economists have therefore traditionally held that because housework is
normally unpaid, it does not create value.

Theorists known as Marxist feminists have countered with the
argument that doing housework can in fact be regarded as producing marketable commodities. What commodities can
housework be said to produce, thereby creating value? The answer
is the housewife's husband and children. The labor power they
represent can be exchanged for wages, which is equivalent to saying they can be sold. Housework then becomes the reproduction
of labor power, of workers, of human beings.

The husband is a worker whose labor can be sold now. The
children are future workers, and to ensure that their labor fetches

a high price, one sends them to good schools. A mother is thus education-minded not only for the children's sake, but also because she wants a high value to be placed on her own labor. If she is to be told "You've done a great job," the child—her product—must graduate from a prestigious school and be hired by a top-ranking company. I am putting it in these terms to illustrate the kind of abstraction one can make in viewing housework as labor—but what I am describing is also a very real facet of everyday life in Japan.

Many Marxist theorists, following Engels in *The Origins of the Family, Private Property*, and the State, distinguish the making of goods (production) and the making of human beings (reproduction, which of course is also the word for procreation of the species). It is tempting to adopt this terminology and define housework as "reproductive labor," and in fact many studies do just that. And yet, confusingly, a "reproductive" task is placed under the rubric of housework only as long as it is performed in the home. Take laundry, cleaning, or cooking: all are examples of labor necessary to support the lives, or the reproduction, of human beings. We would therefore expect them to be "housework" as defined above. But according to everyday usage, the laundry is only housework if a housewife does it at home. When done by a commercial laundry, it becomes ordinary "labor." Accordingly, if I wash a shirt at home, it's housework. If I'm too busy and send the shirt out, it's no longer housework. Likewise with the cooking or the cleaning. Defining housework by equating it with reproductive labor can thus become quite problematical.

THE MARKET AND THE ORIGINS OF HOUSEWORK

The French Marxist feminist Christine Delphy uses a clear and simple formulation which resolves this difficulty: The exclusion of domestic labor from the market is a cause of its being unpaid, not a result.[6] We are accustomed to this idea being put the opposite way. If a mother were asked why she received no wages for cooking the meals and doing the laundry, she might reply "I can't expect to be paid for that because it's housework." Delphy turns this statement on its head and says such work is housework because it is excluded from the market and therefore unpaid. Housework, she says, is merely the name given to that labor which is not incorporated into the market system.

In contemporary life, this definition makes very good sense. An even more striking example than the commercial laundry is the convenience store. There we can purchase a microwaveable meal, practically ready to serve, and lately the store will even heat it up for us. In this case, not only the labor of the factory workers who made the meal but even the pushing of the microwave button by the store employee is paid labor, and therefore not housework. (In the end, eating the meal may well be the last task left unpaid!)

Many tasks that we once automatically thought of as housework are thus turning out not to be. In the final analysis, we cannot distinguish between "housework" and "not housework" by means of job descriptions. Housework, then, is nothing more and nothing less than unpaid labor. Or, to put it another way, labor that is not performed on a market basis.

This brings us to the point of this rather complicated discussion: the key to understanding the nature of housework lies in the concept of the market. The market, as everyone knows, is the system whereby goods and services are bought and sold. Some societies have a highly developed market economy while others do not, with self-sufficiency forming the opposite pole from the market.

We tend to think of housework as timeless. Since human beings have always led some kind of domestic life, surely they must have always done housework to take care of their domestic needs. It is therefore easy to jump to the conclusion that what we call housework is historically older than paid labor. However—and this is a very important point—this conclusion is false. What we know today as housework is quite new, because one cannot distinguish housework from the paid economy until a paid economy has developed. It only becomes possible to identify a particular task as housework in a modern society with a fairly advanced market economy, one in which marketable work can be clearly distinguished from nonmarketable work.

AN EXAMPLE FROM GERMANY

In truth, the formation of market societies and the accompanying birth of housework was a gradual process. There is an excellent study, *Kindai o ikiru onnatachi* (Women's lives in the modern age), which provides a detailed picture of this process.[7] The authors, a group of Japanese researchers, have re-created nineteenth-century German domestic life from a careful reading of diaries, household account books, and other records. They divided the century into two halves and made separate studies of the middle class and the working class in each period.

An early example from the middle class, dating back to the latter half of the eighteenth century, is the housekeeping register of Goethe's childhood home. Goethe's mother was a meticulous bookkeeper, and her highly detailed accounts show that the household purchased vinegar, oil, tea, coffee, sugar, and condiments, but that they smoked their own meats, made their own wine, and bottled their own fruit, cabbage, beans, et cetera. Some goods were bought in a semi-processed state and either finished at home or sent out for finishing. The procedure for making clothes for Goethe's father, an imperial councilor, involved spinning the thread at home, having the cloth woven by a weaver and prepared for sewing by a cutter, and then having it sewn by either a tailor or one of the household servants. There was also a system in which artisans plied their trade from house to house. Some sausage-makers apparently still did this in rural Germany until quite recently, slaughtering the customers' own pigs and turning the meat into sausage on the spot.

The Goethe family's housekeeping demonstrates the complex way in which the purchase of goods and labor on the market combined with home manufacture to support the life of the household. Thus we see that, although housework came into being as the antithesis of the market economy, the process was not a simple one. The scope of housework varied according to how many items were available on the market. By the latter half of the nineteenth century, marketization had progressed and the middle class was buying more of its goods and services.

In the working class, the German archival evidence shows that family life as we know it was virtually nonexistent during the first half of the nineteenth century. At the same time, the middle class presented a model for home life, including housework, and attempted to enlighten the working class. And although so-called enlightenment is not always readily accepted, it seems that the women of the working class gradually came to perceive the middle-class way of life as desirable. Until then they had worked, as a matter of course, in employment of various kinds (mainly as laundresses, housemaids, and other domestic laborers). But from the mid-nineteenth to the early twentieth century, staying at home became the goal for women of the working class also. As their husbands' incomes were not sufficient to support a family, however, they did in fact continue to work after marriage in one form or another. Still, they increasingly identified as housewives and centered their lives on the home as much as possible. They also distanced themselves from the labor movement. In the case of Germany, this process of retreat into the home has been clearly documented.[8]

THE CREATION OF HOME COOKING

To say that housework came into being as a mere surplus or residue of the market does not tell the whole story, however. For it was also actively created by the dissemination of an idealized image of the home which led to raised expectations of domestic life.

For example, Mrs. Beeton's *Book of Household Management* was a best-seller in Victorian England. It was primarily a cookbook, with three-quarters of its pages devoted to recipes. It was by no means the first such collection, since a number of the great chefs of the day had also published books (and Mrs. Beeton was not shy about borrowing their recipes). But the secret of this amateur's success, it is said, was that she chose dishes suited to the tables of the middle class, and that she aimed, above all, to be practical. Her recipes not only gave quantities and cooking times, but listed the costs of the ingredients as well. Mrs. Beeton is often said to have created English home cookery.

Before Mrs. Beeton's day, most people in England ate meals so simple that they hardly qualified as "cookery." Only the gentry dined on dishes that required elaborate preparation. For those who lived on plainer fare, the meal involved next to no "cooking" in the sense of preparation directly before eating.

Actually, food processing once consisted largely of food preservation. Foodstuffs were preserved in a series of regular annual events spread out over the calendar—there was a pickling season, a sausage-making season, and so on. Today, meal preparation is divided into three daily stints just before mealtimes. It was only with the development of the market society, including the technology of transportation and refrigeration, that it became possible to cook a meal from scratch, using fresh meat and vegetables, three times a day—to say, "Let's see, I think I'll make such-and-such tonight." Thus, the very concept of cooking, although it seems entirely natural to us, has only been made possible by our modern social infrastructure.

The dishes Mrs. Beeton recommended to home cooks are said to have had their origins in restaurant food.[9] Restaurant cuisine is regarded today as the opposite of home cooking, and it might be thought to have developed more recently. But, in fact, it was the former private cooks of the French aristocracy, turned out of the manor houses by the revolution, who had the idea of opening restaurants catering to the middle class. There, historians say, their customers tasted "cuisine" for the first time, and home cooking was born when simplified versions of restaurant dishes began to be prepared in bourgeois homes.

Other types of housework which we take for granted also acquired their present form only in modern times. For example, in rural France doing the laundry was a twice-yearly event until the beginning of the twentieth century. When the season arrived, the women of every household, with the help of hired laundresses, spent three days washing the dirty sheets and linen that had accumulated for six months.[10] In time, the frequency of laundering and cleaning rose, together with the standards of cleanliness, as new ideas of hygiene exerted growing influence.

THE TAISHO-PERIOD *OKUSAN*

Let us now turn from European examples back to Japan. When did housework and the housewife become established in this country? In the previous chapter, we noted that it was during the postwar high-growth era that it became a mass phenomenon for women to stay at home, with full-time housewives becoming a majority. But, as in Germany, there were significant class differences. If we look only at the middle class, it seems we can trace the creation of the housewife to the Taisho Period (1912–1926), and particularly to the boom years after the First World War.

Umesao Tadao's article on the superfluous wife theory, quoted earlier, contains a memorable passage related to the advent of the middle-class housewife. The son of a Kyoto merchant family, he writes that his mother was never referred to or addressed as *okusan*. In Kyoto, he recalls, there was no customary term for the wife of the head of a merchant household; instead, she was called by her given name. In nearby Osaka, a merchant's wife was called *oehan or goryonsan* (mistress, proprietress), but never *okusan*. Umesao writes: "To us, *okusan* meant a woman who lived in cheaply built rental housing for civil servants or the like, fancied herself better than shopkeepers, and always beat their prices down using superior tones. In our eyes, she did nothing during the day but chatter with her other *okusan* neighbors. And indeed it was true that the wives of low-level salaried employees—policemen, teachers, and office workers—liked to call one another *okusan*."

In premodern times, this name had designated married women of the warrior class; now, it was coming to mean the wife of a salaried employee. I noted earlier that women became housewives en masse as the base of Japan's social structure shifted to the company employee following the Second World War. This trend had its roots in the Taisho Period, when the economic boom and rapid industrialization which followed the First World War generated a whole new class of what we would now call white-collar workers, those who did the administrative work of large organizations.

Together with teachers and government employees, these office workers are known as "the new middle class," as opposed to the old middle class of merchants like Umesao's family. This new middle class created a new lifestyle: that is, they moved to the residential suburbs which were being developed on the outskirts of large cities, and from there the husbands commuted to their downtown offices on the newly built streetcar lines. With this separation of workplace and home, and thus of the public and private realms, wives of this class took on the title of the cloistered *okusan*, who had looked after the domestic affairs in her husband's absence.

But were the *okusan* of the new middle class living the same kind of life as today's housewives do? Not in one very important respect.

Figure 2-1 shows a typical example of suburban middle-class housing of the Taisho Period, a house designed around a central corridor. In contrast to traditional domestic architecture, in which

Fig. 2-1. Central-corridor housing plan

Design by Kenmotsu Hatsujiro, awarded first prize in a 1917 contest sponsored by Jyutaku (Housing) magazine. Total floor area: 101 square meters. Figures in plan are areas in standard tatami units (0.9 × 1.8m).

Source: Reprinted from Nishikawa Yuko, "Sumai no hensen to 'katei' no seiritsu" (Changes in housing and the formation of "the home").[11]

the rooms interconnected directly, this plan is characterized by the independence of the rooms which open off the central corridor. It is also characterized by the separation made between the internal public space (the parlor with attached study which can be reached directly from the entrance), and the family's living space.[11] These features reflected the development of the new idea of family privacy.

In comparison to contemporary Japanese homes, we find several major differences. For one thing, a study or parlor has now become a luxury. But the most noticeable difference is the maid's room. No house built today would contain one.

In the Taisho Period, as this typical house plan tells us, middle-class Japanese commonly hired a domestic worker, known as a *jochu* (maid). In this they resembled the middle classes of nineteenth-century Europe. The range of housework in those days was much wider than it is today. Kimono and futon covers were made at home, and had to be taken apart for cleaning, washed, and stretched on frames to dry. Fuel had to be prepared for the bath and the charcoal braziers, and foodstuffs had to be preserved by such methods as pickling or drying. Moreover, standards were on the rise due to the increasing influence of new concepts of hygiene and the demand for greater comfort. The amount of work and the prevailing standards of cleanliness were such that the housewife could not possibly cope on her own; thus, the presence of domestic help was indispensable. However, unless the family owned rental property or had other sources of income, the husband's earnings had to be sufficient to cover all the household expenses if the wife was to stay at home full-time. According to a study based on household budget surveys conducted by government statisticians, in the Meiji Period (1868–1912) only civil servants and the upper ranks of company employees earned enough for their wives to stay at home. By mid-Taisho, however, the incomes of both office and factory workers were steadily increasing, and in the early years of the Showa Period (1926–1989), civil servants, teachers, office workers, and factory workers had all attained the necessary income level.[12] Although in the poorest stratum of Japanese society both husband and wife continued to work after this time, it should be noted that, on the whole, there seems to have been less difference between the classes in this respect in Japan than there was in Europe, at least as far down the scale as the urban factory worker.

SYNONYMOUS WITH WOMANHOOD

The modernized houses of the Taisho Period were replaced by multi-unit housing complexes as the typical accommodation of post-World War II families. As rapid economic growth brought an influx of young people to the urban centers, many—especially among the educated white-collar class—settled in the publicly subsidized suburban developments known as *danchi*. According to the *White Paper on the National Life* for 1960, their consumption patterns included a liking for more Western-style foods, such as meat, milk, eggs, fruit, and bread, as well as the purchase of many home appliances.[13] By the 1960s, maids—or housekeepers, as they had been known since the war—had almost completely disappeared. The postwar housewife donned a smock or apron while at home and did all the cleaning, washing, shopping, and cooking by the sweat of her own brow. But she could not lower the standards for housework, which had been raised while employing a maid; instead, various electrical appliances came to take the place of hired help.

Apart from not having servants, postwar housewives differed from the prewar *okusan* in another important respect, namely, their greater numbers relative to the total population of Japanese women. I regard this point as far more than a simple matter of numbers, because majority status makes a crucial difference to a group's power to define the norm. Before the war, there was a diversity of images of women besides the *okusan*. Women filled a variety of social niches, including the yome or hardworking young daughter-in-law in a farming household, and the merchant family's *goryonsan*. The *okusan* was just one among many. From the different vantage point of the *goryonsan*, for instance, the *okusan* became the target of caustic criticism for doing nothing but chatter during the daytime.

After the war, however, with housewives overwhelmingly in the majority, it was the merchants' and farmers' wives and the professional women who came to feel socially inferior, because the value system now in the ascendant said that it was better to "do nothing" during the day—better, that is, to devote oneself to housework and child rearing.

In the postwar period, the state of being a housewife became so strongly normative that it was practically synonymous with womanhood. As we have seen, however, being a housewife had not always been the expected way of life for every woman.

Chapter 3 | The Two-Child Revolution

THE GENERATION OF "THE METAL BAT MURDERS"

In 1980, a young man in Kawasaki was attending cram school for a second year after failing his university entrance exams. One day in November he clubbed his sleeping parents to death with a metal baseball bat. The incident, which came to be known as "the metal bat murders," received a great deal of media attention, and many readers in Japan will no doubt recall it still. What makes the incident stick in my mind is the feeling that that could have been me with the bat. I know this is a strange and rather alarming thing to say, so let me put it another way: I felt that I belonged to the same generation.

He and I were only two years apart in age. The photographs of his home which appeared in the weekly magazines showed the sort of ordinary house often pictured in Realtors' ads, and it seems to have contained an ordinary middle-class family, one to which I could readily relate. The parents had high expectations of their son. His father, in particular, stressed educational achievement, and this was said to have led to the murders. If one thinks of the killer as the child of an ordinary middle-class family, whose parents loved him and expected him to succeed, it may seem a senseless crime. But I felt I understood it very well, and so did my friends. We all knew the pressures a child of an ordinary middle-class family felt. One of my friends went so far as to say, "I wonder if anyone grows up these days without wanting, at least once, to kill their parents."

My project of reexamining the postwar family from a woman's perspective is, of course, related to my own experience as a woman in a postwar family, and, accordingly, in the first two chapters I have specifically been looking at the situation of the housewife. But I am also the child of a postwar family, one of those supposedly spoiled children who grew up in the midst of material affluence and never wanted for anything. My experience tells me that even with this affluence, those children grew up with a stifling sense of being wrapped in cotton wool and having no escape. Perhaps it would be more accurate to say, then, that I am reexamining the postwar family from the perspectives of both women and children.

TWO DROPS IN THE BIRTHRATE

In this chapter, then, we will turn our attention to children and what I call "the two-child revolution." Japan's falling birthrate has recently been causing much concern. The total fertility rate reached 1.57 in 1990, giving rise to the expression "the 1.57 shock," since this figure was beneath even the historic low of 1.58 recorded in 1966 (an anomaly due, as we shall see, to the effects of a superstitious belief that 1966 was an unlucky year). The rate then continued to decrease, falling to 1.53 in 1991, and reaching a new low of 1.46 in 1993 before recovering slightly to 1.50 in 1994.

The total fertility rate (TFR) in a particular year is an estimate of the total number of children one hypothetical woman is expected to bear in her lifetime, assuming that the age-specific fertility rates of that year remain constant throughout the woman's reproductive life. The population will more or less reproduce itself if each woman has two children. Actually, when we allow for those children who die before reaching reproductive age, each woman must bear about 2.1 children if the existing population level is to be maintained. This is called the replacement level.

The fact that the total fertility rate is now far below this level means that Japan's population is expected to decline, much to the consternation of the government and the press. Let us review the

figures which are attracting so much attention and see how they
have changed over the postwar period.

In figure 3-1, the lower line shows changes in the crude
birthrate (CBR), that is, the number of live births per year per
thousand population, and the upper line shows the total fertility
rates (TFR). It is better to use the TFR in order to exclude the
effects of changes in the population's age structure; essentially,
though, the shape of the postwar trends remains the same. When
we look at the period since 1945, it is clear that there have actually been not one but two drops in the birthrate. Before the war
there was also a more gradual downtrend, commencing in the
Taisho Period (1912–26), but it was not until the postwar era that
the decline was fully realized.

On closer examination, a more complex pattern of change
emerges. In spite of the wartime policy expressed by the slogan
"*umeyo fuyaseyo*" (Have children! Boost the population!), the
birthrate did not rise during World War II. Following a universal
law of war, when the men returned from the front and all those

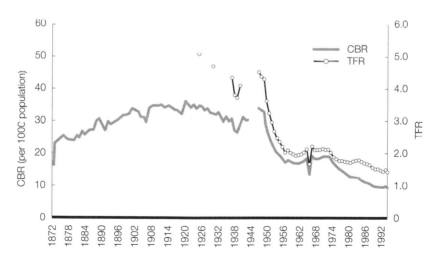

**Fig. 3-1. Long-term trends of birthrates in Japan, 1872–1995
(Crude birthrates and total fertility rates)**

Sources: Prepared from Institute of Population Problems, Ministry of Health and Welfare, *Jinko no doko:
Nihon to sekai* (Population trends: Japan and the world), 1988 and 1996 editions. Data from
Cabinet Bureau of Statistics, *Nihon teikoku nenkan* (Yearbook of Imperial Japan), and Statistics and
Information Department, Ministry of Health and Welfare, *Jinko dotai tokei* (Vital Statistics).

who had been waiting to have children could do so at last, there was a baby boom which appears on the graph as a steep peak from 1947 to 1949. The people born in these three years have been named the *dankai no sedai* or "clumped generation," the Japanese equivalent of "baby boomers," though this term as it is used in Europe and America is generally associated with a longer period of time.

Japan's baby boom lasted only until 1949. Immediately thereafter, in what I will call "the first decline," the birthrate dropped as suddenly as a roller coaster and continued in free fall for eight years. Then—and I would like to draw particular attention to this fact—the birthrate more or less leveled off. The sharp drop in 1966 is discounted for purposes of observing trends as this was *hinoe uma* (the year of the fire-horse), the 43rd year in the 60-year cycle of the Chinese zodiac. Women born in *hinoe uma* were traditionally regarded as bringers of misfortune to their husbands, and couples avoided having a child during this year.

The birthrate began its second decline in the mid-1970s. This is the decline currently attracting a great deal of attention. The graph makes it clear, however, that in its overall downward movement Japan's postwar birthrate has passed through three stages—two declines with an intervening period of stability.

In chapter 1, I noted that the postwar era has not been a time of uniform change in one direction. The birthrate graph shows more clearly that there have been various turning points along the way. What we generally think of as the postwar period took on its characteristic profile rapidly, that is, by the mid-fifties, and this profile was then maintained over a long period of stability during which the birthrate remained level. This quintessential postwar period was the era when women were housewives and couples had two or three children: the sort of family that, even today, probably comes most readily to mind when one thinks of "the family."

In this and succeeding chapters, I plan to review the period from 1945 to the present day in three stages: first, the preparatory stage in which the postwar structure was formed; then the two decades of stability which typify the postwar period, from about 1955 to 1975; and finally, the period in which the stable structure broke down or changed. I propose to apply this three-stage scheme not only to the birthrate but also to broader changes in the family and the relationships between women, men, and children.

THE TWO-CHILD REVOLUTION

Just as we went back to the origins of the housewife to gain insight into how the postwar structure developed, in this chapter we will look closely at the implications of the first decline in the birthrate. The speed of this decline was striking in comparison with those nations which had modernized before Japan. What happened to produce a drop in the birthrate so steep that it could be called an event in world history?

Table 3-1 shows the number of children borne by married women grouped according to their own year of birth, a grouping which is known as a "birth cohort." The term "cohort" basically means the same as "generation" but has a more formal definition: it means a group of persons who have experienced the same life

Table 3-1. Number of children ever born to married women, by woman's birth cohort

Year of woman's birth	Number of children					Average no. of children ever born
	0	1	2	3	4 or more	
	Percentage of women with no. of children shown above					
pre-1890 (pre-Meiji 24)	11.8	6.8	6.6	8.0	66.8	4.96
1891–1895 (Meiji 24–28)	10.1	7.3	6.8	7.6	68.1	5.07
1896–1900 (Meiji 29–33)	9.4	7.6	6.9	8.3	67.9	5.03
1901–1905 (Meiji 34–38)	8.6	7.5	7.4	9.0	67.4	4.99
1911–1915 (Meiji 44–Taisho 4)	7.1	7.9	9.4	13.8	61.8	4.18
1921–1925 (Taisho 10–14)	6.9	9.2	24.5	29.7	29.6	2.86
1928–1932 (Showa 3–7)	3.6	11.0	47.0	29.0	9.4	2.33
1933–1937 (Showa 8–12)	3.6	10.8	54.2	25.7	5.7	2.21
1938–1942 (Showa 13–17)	3.6	10.3	55.0	25.5	5.5	2.20
1943–1947 (Showa 18–22)	3.8	8.9	57.0	23.9	5.0	2.18

Sources: Prepared from Institute of Population Problems, Ministry of Health and Welfare, *Jinko no doko: Nihon to sekai* (Population trends: Japan and the world), 1996 edition, Table 4-26. Data from Statistics Bureau, Management and Coordination Agency, *Kokusei chosa hokoku* (National census report), and Institute of Population Problems, Ministry of Health and Welfare, *Shussanryoku chosa* (Survey of fertility) and *Shussei doko kihon chosa* (Basic survey of birth trends).

event (in this case, who were born) during a specified period. We similarly speak of marriage cohorts, etc. (The word "generation," on the other hand, is used more loosely, referring sometimes to one step in the line of descent from parents to offspring, and sometimes to shared historical experience, e.g., "the war generation," "the postwar generation," "the Security Treaty protest generation," or "the jaded generation.")

Table 3-1 thus shows the distribution of number of children by birth cohort of women who were ever married.[1] We note first that in the upper five cohorts, consisting of women who were born during the Meiji (1868–1912) and early Taisho (1912–26) Periods, the majority had four or more children. The distribution begins to change with the women born in 1921–25, and by the time we come to the 1928–32 birth cohort, women with only two or three children are by far the biggest group. It was these women, born in the early years of the Showa Period (1926–89), who established the pattern of childbearing that has remained largely unchanged until our own time. This is the group which married shortly after the end of the war, and the birthrate took its roller coaster plunge as they began having children. It is sometimes said of the first generation to marry after the war that it was they who changed the family, and it was certainly they who gave postwar society the form it retained right up to the 1970s. They may not have had the style and fervor of those who would later take to the streets or shut down campuses in political protest, but nevertheless they may have been the most revolutionary generation in postwar Japan.

In that spirit, I have renamed the first decline in the birthrate "the two-child revolution." It seems, however, that a decrease in the number of children per couple was not the only factor at work. Note the percentages on the left of table 3-1, representing women who bore no children. Given that the average number of children decreased, we might reasonably expect that more women would have no children, but in fact the opposite is true: whereas about 10 percent of Meiji women who had ever married had no children, in the early Showa cohorts this figure shrank by more than half. Thus, while there was a steep reduction in the average number of children per couple from 1950 to 1957, the picture is not complete until we add that at the same time there was also an increase in the uniformity of the number of children that couples had.

In the last chapter, we observed a similar standardization as it became usual for women to be housewives, and as, moreover, the value system associated with the majority declared this to be women's proper role. The same can be said of family size: two or three children became very much the norm, the *right* number to have. Viewed in this light, the postwar family begins to look highly standardized, as if it were adhering to a rigid notion of what being a family means.

ABORTION BEFORE CONTRACEPTION

When the birthrate plummeted, how was fertility being controlled? Today the principal method used in Japan is contraception, but for a time after the war it was abortion. Although the 1907 law which criminalized abortion has never been repealed, the 1948 Eugenic Protection Law effectively liberalized abortion by recognizing economic grounds. This measure preceded the legal reforms of the 1970s in Europe and the United States, but it was not adopted out of respect for a woman's right to choose; rather, it was a measure for population control adopted in response to food shortages in the aftermath of the war. Although Japan still utilizes abortion as a means of birth control to a greater extent than Europe or the United States,[2] its proportional level has decreased considerably since those years, when it was used more often than contraception. Figure 3-2 shows the trends of reported induced abortions in postwar Japan, and table 3-2 shows estimates of the proportions of total pregnancies theoretically expected that were averted by contraception and by induced abortion, or that resulted in births actually recorded.[3]

On an outlying island off Shikoku, I once interviewed an elderly woman about childbirth.[4] She spoke of having had as many as five or six abortions, which she induced herself. And these were all pregnancies *in* wedlock. She told me that condoms had been available cheaply through programs to encourage birth control,

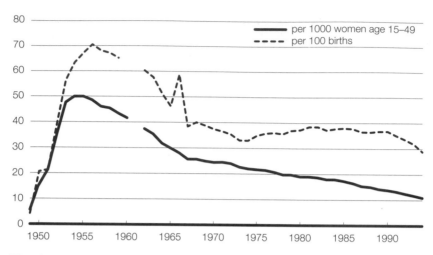

Fig. 3-2. Report induced abortion rates in Japan, 1949–94

Note: The sudden rise in 1966 was due to the low number of births during *hinoe uma* (year of the fire-horse).
Sources: Prepared from Institute of Population Problems, Ministry of Health and Welfare, *Jinko no doko:
Nihon to sekai* (Population trends: Japan and the world), 1996 edition, Table 4-19. Data from
Statistics and Information Department, Ministry of Health and Welfare, *Eisei nenpo* (Annual report on
public health) and *Yuseihogo tokei hokoku* (Statistical report on eugenic protection).

**Table 3-2. Births actually recorded, averted by induced abortion
and by contraception in Japan, 1955–1970
(per 100 pregnancies theoretically expected)**

	Proportion of births actually recorded	Proportion of births averted by ind. abort.	Proportion of births averted by contraception
1955	44.9	37.4	17.7
1960	38.8	31.4	29.8
1965	38.2	19.8	42.0
1970	38.3	16.9	44.3

Sources: From Muramatsu Minoru, "Abortion in Modern Japan," presented to the IUSSP and IRCJS
Workshop on Abortion, Infanticide and Neglect in Asian History held in Kyoto, 1994.

because after the war it was government policy to limit the population. But she couldn't bear to use them. She would have been too ashamed. She couldn't bring herself to ask her husband to wear one, and he clearly didn't like the idea. It was altogether just too shameful to have sex like that—so much so that she would even rather have had an abortion.

Although what people do in bed has not been as constant through the ages as one might think, there is great resistance at first to doing something differently. And this couple's resistance to practicing birth control was very strong. But, she told me, by the time she had had five or six abortions, her husband grew concerned for her health and started using condoms.

The steep decline in the birthrate was achieved by aborting almost as many fetuses as were carried to term, doing violence to women's bodies and to their hearts. And yet, during those years, the government actively pursued the lower birthrates obtained by this means. Then in the 1970s, when the birthrate had in their estimation fallen too far, some members of the Diet began to invoke the concept of respect for life. However, it should not be forgotten that Japan's lawmakers have continually sought to place both the lives of fetuses and women's bodies at the service of the current demands of population policy.

CHILDREN AS CONSUMER DURABLES

To return to the trends we have observed: why did the number of children become smaller and more uniform? In general, why does this number decrease with modernization? In chapter 1, we saw that the puzzle of why women became housewives as the society modernized could be explained by the conversion of the industrial structure. The same explanation also applies in this case. In essence, in the transformation from an agricultural to a white-collar society, the value of children changed.

In an agricultural society, children are, economically speaking, "producer goods." In an industrial society, where most workers are employees, children become "consumer goods." The former may be defined as goods (such as factory machinery) which are used to produce other goods, while the latter, like our food and clothing, are simply used, period.

In agricultural societies, children are "producer goods" in that they help on the family farm after being supported for a number of years. Modern-day children, however, generally do not provide any economic return to their parents, even when they reach maturity. Most work for a corporate employer rather than the family business, and their earnings are spent on their own needs. Parents may hope to be looked after in their old age, but they cannot count on it. Children no longer produce value in the future. They are now "consumer goods," simply to be used up.

As for what they are used for, one can only conclude that it is enjoyment. Children are cute. They can be a lot of fun. Some people would say they stay cute for three years, some would say ten. To parents today, children are essentially consumer durables which provide pleasure for a certain number of years. As such, they are not unlike refrigerators, televisions, or washing machines. This may seem a shocking analogy, but in practice, economists such as Gary Becker treat children as exactly this kind of factor in order to estimate birthrates. These economists say that if they treat children as consumer goods and introduce them into the equations used to predict a couple's purchases of refrigerators, cars, and so on, they can obtain quite valid estimates of how many children the couple will have.[5]

But while this model may, in part, explain the decrease in the number of children per couple—because, in an economic sense, children became costs and not gains—it cannot account for the standardization of this number. The pleasure that people obtain from, say, a TV set or a car presumably varies according to individual taste, so that some people spend a fortune buying a car, while others go in for the latest audiovisual equipment. There should thus have been nothing wrong with someone saying, "Instead of having children, I plan to keep buying expensive foreign cars, one after another, all my life." Or "I like to travel abroad every year, so I won't be able to afford children, and anyway, they'd only get in the way." Yet everyone continued to have a very similar number of children; moreover, the number of children per couple has generally tended not to fall below two. This was long considered especially true of Japan. Despite strong disincentives in the form of high education and housing costs, the number of children per married couple did not fall consistently below two until the generation of parents now in their fifties.[6]

Thus there was evidently more to this phenomenon than can be explained by equating children with consumer goods. One begins to suspect that the social norm which said that it took two or three children to make one's family and one's life complete may have prevented the number of children falling any lower for economic reasons, and thus may have been responsible for the standardization of family size.

THE BIRTH OF "THE CHILD"

Let us turn our attention, then, from economic factors to the realm of norms or meanings. What implications did the decrease in family size have for children, and for parents? The reason people had fewer children was not because they valued them less; on the contrary, it seems that people limited their families so that they could love the children they had all the more.

For a historian, to trace something as intangible as feelings toward children is an extremely difficult task, but there is one man, the French social historian Philippe Ariès, whose pioneering work elevated such research to a new historical science. His 1960 classic was titled *L'enfant et la vie familiale sous l'ancien régime*. It was published in English as *Centuries of Childhood: A Social History of Family Life*, and in Japanese as *"Kodomo" no tanjo* (The birth of "the child").[7] The book has had such an impact on the fields of education and family history that they are virtually divided into pre-Ariès and post-Ariès epochs. This kind of approach, the study of the world view and emotional life of a particular age, is known as the history of *mentalité*.

The Japanese title "The Birth of 'The Child'" denotes not an actual birth but the evolution of a concept—"the child," in quotation marks. Ariès says that at one time "the child" did not exist, that the concept came into being at a certain point in history.

One may well object that children are visibly different from adults, that childhood is a biological fact not subject to historical change. But think of all the young people in many societies today who have grown to their full height—often taller than their parents—and can even have children themselves, and yet their own consciousness and our social arrangements say that they are children. The boundary line of childhood is a social convention, not a biologically determined fact.

Until the end of the Middle Ages a child was regarded as a small adult. For as soon as it had passed the helpless stage of infancy and could feed and dress itself and attend to its own excretory functions, the child mingled, worked, and played with adults. In fact, children played by imitating adults at work.

According to Ariès, it was not until the seventeenth century that children came to be regularly portrayed in paintings as charming little figures. The important event of this period was that the children of the middle class began to go to school. They thus entered a distinct phase of life known as "childhood," a period of preparation after passing through infancy and before commencing work. Childhood arrived first for boys, because at first it was only boys who went to school. Ariès notes that it was boys of school age who were first dressed in clothing that separated them from adults.[8]

As "the child" came to be regarded as a distinct entity which was innocent and pure, the idea developed that adults should both cherish children and provide them with education—things which required money and effort. The number of children per couple thus came to be limited to two or three because children had become cherished beings, and also because the cost of supporting them to adulthood had increased.

THE BIRTH OF THE MOTHER

The birth of "the child" inevitably brought changes to parents also, and there are historians who, modeling their work on Ariès, argue for a conceptual birth of "the mother." One of them is Elisabeth Badinter, author of *L'amour en plus*.[9] Badinter takes up factual evidence showing that in eighteenth-century Paris only one thousand of the babies born in a year were raised on their mothers' milk. A further one thousand were suckled by wet nurses in the parental home. The remaining nineteen thousand babies born each year were taken away and placed with foster parents in rural areas near Paris. Many of these infants died, having been placed out at a very tender age and under conditions which did not guarantee the best of care from their foster parents.

We can readily imagine the sorrow and anger of those who lost their children in this way, but in fact they seem to have been less moved than we might think. The historical records paint a picture of parents resigning themselves to their loss immediately on hearing the news, making no effort to investigate the cause of death, and telling themselves that the child had gone to join the angels in Heaven. Such evidence implies that parents did not have as strong an emotional attachment to their children as they do today.

Badinter's theory that premodern mothers lacked mother love has aroused much controversy. For example, Linda Pollock's *Forgotten Children* marshals evidence to the contrary in the form of excerpts from diaries and letters in which parents express their love for their children.[10]

In my view, the most significant work in this area is the opposing argument put forward by Françoise Loux, author of *Le jeune enfant et son corps dans la médicine traditionelle*.[11] Among the practices she examines is swaddling, or wrapping an infant's body in narrow strips of cloth like bandages. In the eighteenth century, this custom was attacked by advocates of new methods of child rearing, including Jean-Jacques Rousseau. They deplored it as insanitary, since the swaddling clothes could not easily be changed when soiled, and also as cruelly restrictive of the child's freedom. But Loux gathered oral histories from old women who, as young mothers, had still swaddled their babies at the turn of this century, and discovered that they did so in the belief that the child's body would be poorly developed unless it was "formed" and corrected in this way.

The child-rearing methods of an earlier time appear callous to us because they are founded on concepts of the body and of life which are completely different from those we hold today. But in any such discussion it is important to remember that then, as now, parents were most likely doing what they thought was good for their children.

When we compare premodern and modern mothers, however, there is an obvious difference which, I believe, should be emphasized more than issues concerning mother love. For although we are now quite accustomed to hearing it said that motherhood is a woman's highest calling and a mother's love the noblest of all emotions, when first propounded by Rousseau and others in the eighteenth century, this was received as a novel and not altogether pleasing idea.

For example, Balzac's novel *Le contrat du mariage* (The marriage contract) contains a scene in which a mother tells her daughter what she should know about married life on the eve of her wedding to a young aristocrat. It is exactly the opposite of the advice a modern mother might be expected to give: "The cause of the undoing of married women bent upon retaining their husbands' hearts . . . is their constant contact, which did not exist in the old days but was introduced into this country with the family mania. Since the French Revolution, bourgeois customs have invaded aristocratic circles. This sad state of affairs is due to one of their writers, Rousseau. . . . And since then, women in the best society have nursed their own children, educated their daughters themselves, and remained at home. Thus, life is so complicated that happiness has become almost impossible."[12]

Like daughters today, however, young women in eighteenth-century France did not meekly follow their parents' advice. Informing Mother that she was old-fashioned, and that nursing one's own baby was the latest thing, the daughters of the minor aristocracy and the bourgeoisie took to domesticity. They were part of a trend which would eventually establish motherhood as the unquestioned norm of female identity. The idea of family came to mean, by definition, the mother devoting herself to the care of two or three children and lovingly nurturing them with her own hands. This was the image of the family which modern society came to idealize and embrace most ardently.

LOVE AS A FORM OF CONTROL

Modern children may be thought lucky to have such great social value attached to maternal love. But there is another side to the story. In 1979, a Japanese pediatrician named Kyotoku Shigemori published a best-seller with the sensational title *Bogenbyo*, a word he coined that meant "maternally induced diseases."[13] In this book, the author argues that, beginning in the late 1950s, the illnesses contracted by Japanese children changed. Prior to that time they suffered mostly from contagious diseases—stomach upsets, respiratory illnesses, and so on. These became less prevalent, however, due to the overall improvement of sanitation and the trend to smaller families in which each child received more parental attention. But the hope that children in the future would be free of illness was short-lived, for there was soon an upsurge of illnesses of a different type: bronchial asthma, stammering, poor appetite, school phobia, and proneness to bone fractures, to name just a few.

Kyutoku states outright that the pathogen responsible in all these cases was the children's mothers. (It should be noted here that I disagree with this emphasis on the mother as sole cause, a point I will discuss further in chapter 8.) For example, he says, he had noticed that mothers who brought their children to be treated for asthma fell into two broad types. "One is the overprotective mother, who makes her child bundle up warmly when the weather's a little chilly, and won't let the child take a bath if it has a bit of a runny nose. The other is the scolding mother, who reprimands her child severely for the slightest mischief and crushes the child by telling it to be good and be quiet."[14] These ways of handling children, Kyutoku suggested, were causing illnesses linked with psychological problems.

"Maternally induced illnesses have become especially conspicuous in recent years, since about the middle of the 1950s, rising parallel to the curve of Japan's modern civilization and GNP growth," he wrote.[15] It was in the mid-1950s that the birthrate underwent its first decline and the average number of children per couple fell to slightly more than two. It thus seems to me very suggestive that these children, who were essentially the first offspring of the Postwar Family System, were also the first to develop illnesses which could be characterized in this way.

Postwar mothers have been devoting their attention to a smaller number of children, and furthermore they have been doing so full-time. Having given up any other life they might have had, they have made their children their reason for living. This may seem a boon for the child, but the corollary is that the child must live up to being its mother's purpose in life.

Moreover, modern mothers also serve as proxies for two major institutions. The first is the medical profession: with the advent of modern ideas about hygiene, people have become very particular about minute details of daily life. Mothers are always reminding the whole family—husbands, too—to wash their hands, eat the right foods, and so on. They were first called on to perform this role of preventers of disease in the eighteenth and nineteenth centuries.[16]

Secondly, of course, mothers also act as proxies for the school teacher. Together, public health and education are the central means of institutional control in modern society, a control which penetrates to people's innermost lives. It is perhaps not surprising that mothers, as the producers of human life, have been led to believe that it is their duty to carry out these functions. In the name of love, mothers become the unwitting local agents of authority in the home, enforcing societal control over their children.

Thus, in the generation of the metal bat murders, an emotional conflict quietly spread among the children of the two-child family. While happily receiving and returning their parents' love, it seems that they also harbored the feeling, somewhere in their hearts, that the only way to throw off the oppressively heavy burden of that love would be to kill their parents.

REPRODUCTIVE EGALITARIANISM

I would like to conclude this discussion with an international comparison, as I did in chapter 1, in order to situate postwar Japan in a broader perspective. In Europe, a major demographic change equivalent to Japan's postwar two-child revolution occurred in the late nineteenth and early twentieth centuries. This change is known as the "fertility transition."

France began to experience a falling birthrate long before the rest of Europe. A gradual decline began directly after the Revolution which Rousseau had helped bring about. The method of birth control used at that time is known to have been the simple one of withdrawal, or coitus interruptus. It is interesting to note that the French Revolution heralded or, rather, paralleled, a change in sexual behavior.

In the other European nations, the downward trend began almost a century later, during the last two or three decades of the 1800s, and took forty to fifty years to reach its lowest point.

In discussing fertility in Europe—or any society, for that matter—we must take into account its relationship with the marriage rate or, more precisely, the rate of nuptiality based on *de facto* as well as legal marital status. The fertility (birthrate) of a particular society can be expressed by the following equation:

Fertility = marriage rate × marital fertility

　　　　+ (1– marriage rate)× extramarital fertility

where "marriage" and "marital" refer to established relationships of de facto as well as legal status. Since the probability of giving birth without having an established partner is very low in any society, it is possible to omit the second part of the equation, leaving:

Fertility ≒ marriage rate × marital fertility

These elements express the two conditions necessary for children to be born. Conversely, the fertility of a society will be reduced not only when the birthrate per couple is limited, but also when men and women form couples at a slower rate.

Marriage in Northwestern Europe, at least after the sixteenth century, exhibited a set of distinct characteristics known as the "European marriage pattern."[17] The first characteristic was the late timing of marriage, at an average age of 25 or 26 for women and 27 or 28 for men. The second was that it was less than universal. The rate of lifelong celibacy was exceptionally high compared to other preindustrial societies, with over 10 percent of both men and women remaining unmarried all their lives. The existence of alternatives, including the monastic life and the practice of young people entering service in other households for extended periods, acted to hold down the marriage rate.

With this in mind, it is interesting to note the number of European thinkers who never married, among them Descartes and Kant. This is believed to reflect the clerical tradition in European intellectual history, and it has also been suggested that, for the same reason, European philosophy is essentially misogynistic and phallocentric in nature.

Be that as it may, the characteristic European marriage pattern disintegrated dramatically between about 1930 and 1940. In both Northwestern and Southern Europe, there was an almost simultaneous shift toward early and universal marriage, resulting in a sharp rise in marriage rates.

Interestingly, marital fertility, which had been declining steeply throughout Europe since the 1870s, reached its lowest point in this same decade. It was as if a new enthusiasm for marriage had been released as marital fertility came to be controlled.[18] Europe was in transition from a society in which not all of the population married but those who did had many children, to a society where everyone married, but everyone limited their family.

We could perhaps call a society in which everyone married and produced two or three children a society of "reproductive egalitarianism." Modern societies, or, to be precise, twentieth-century industrialized societies, have all at one time been societies of "reproductive egalitarianism."

I have already mentioned that Japan's two-child revolution involved both a reduction and a standardization of the number of children per couple, but we must also take note of the marriage rate. The fertility transition in Europe and the United States was accompanied by a rise in marriage rates; in other words, everyone had a chance to marry. Egalitarianism in marriage was also seen in postwar Japanese society, although the marriage rate did not rise to any significant degree. Figure 3-3 shows the average age at first marriage in Japan. From this graph, we learn that during the period of about 20 years (from about 1955 to 1975) which I have said typifies the postwar period, the average age at first marriage was stable. It should also be noted that during this period the variance of age at first marriage was low, indicating that the norm of the *tekireiki*, or "appropriate age for marriage," was strongly binding.

Marriageable women in Japan used to be compared to Christmas cakes: it's hard to find a taker after (Dec.) 24. This bad joke certainly had a point during the typical postwar decades,

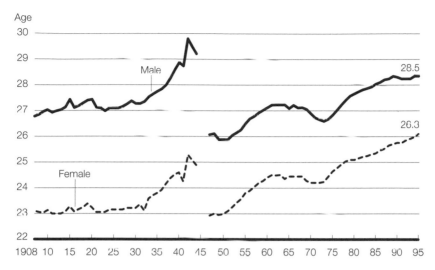

Fig. 3-3. Age at first marriage in Japan, 1908–1995

Sources: Adapted, with additional data, from Inoue Teruko et al., ed., *Josei no detabukku* (Women's
databook), 2nd edition (Tokyo: Yuhikaku, 1995), Fig. 5-1. Data from Statistics and Information
Department, Ministry of Health and Welfare, *Jinko dotai tokei* (Vital Statistics).

when most women married by 24, became full-time housewives,
and had a family of two or three children whom they both loved
and controlled. While the reproductive egalitarianism of those
years could be seen as giving people an equal opportunity to leave
descendants of their own, at the same time it was a nightmarish
era which imposed a uniform life course on every man and every
woman. Perhaps the conformism for which the Japanese have such
a reputation has unexpectedly shallow historical roots: it may
have been greatly intensified, if not actually created, during the
postwar period.

Chapter 4 | The Truth about the Nuclearization of the Family

THE NOSTALGIC APPEAL OF *SAZAE-SAN*

I often keep my daughter company watching cartoons on TV. Sunday night is time for *Sazae-san*. This series features the doings of housewife Sazae, her husband Masuo, and their son Tara-chan, who live together with Sazae's parents, the Isonos, and her younger brother and sister. Another favorite of ours is *Chibi Maruko-chan* (Little Maruko) about a girl and her family—mother, father, sister, and paternal grandparents.

Sakura Momoko, the creator of Little Maruko, belongs to almost the same generation as I do. Since Maruko was modeled on Ms. Sakura's own childhood, the school scenes and the atmosphere of the town evoke a great deal of nostalgia in me. They capture a sense of the sixties and early seventies down to the minutest detail.

Sazae-san, whose devotees have put out volumes of research, has been running for so many years that its sense of a particular era has become a little blurred. Things that appear in the Isono household sometimes seem strangely up-to-date when one considers that the original comic strip was first published in 1946. On the whole, though, *Sazae-san* retains a strong flavor of the fifties and sixties.

There are many fans of both *Sazae-san* and *Chibi Maruko-chan* among the college students I teach. When I ask them why they enjoy these shows, they tell me, "I miss families like that—they seem like real families." Sometimes they add, "You don't often see that kind of family these days." This reply strikes me as puzzling: why do my students feel nostalgia for an era before they were born? What do families from the sixties mean to them?

One point we should note about both cartoon series is that the families they portray consist of three generations living together. We will look into the reasons for this in this chapter.

Before exploring these questions, let us briefly review our findings so far. In chapters 1 and 2 we looked at the origins of the housewife prior to World War II, and traced the trend which led to a majority of women taking on this role full-time during the era of high economic growth—a trend which, as you will recall, was eventually reversed. In chapter 3 we saw that the postwar decline in the birthrate took place in two stages, with an intervening period of stability from about 1955 to 1975. Thus, in areas related to both women and children, we traced the emergence after the war of a stable structure which was maintained for an extended period of time before eventually breaking down again. This is the structure I have named "the Postwar Family System." Both *Sazae-san* and *Chibi Maruko-chan* are set in exactly the era when this structure was firmly in place and the postwar family boasted an unshakable stability.

FROM THE *IE* TO THE NUCLEAR FAMILY

We will examine the Postwar Family System in detail in chapter 5. But first, let us pause to consider a more familiar explanation of postwar changes in the family. We are accustomed to hearing these changes described primarily in terms of liberation from the traditional *ie* system together with a movement toward the nuclear family. Where do these two issues fit into the picture we have seen so far? Can the postwar history of the family be viewed as a process of transition from the *ie* to the nuclear family?

A brief outline of the *ie* system may be in order here. Though often translated as "family," the *ie* is closer in concept to the English term "household," and closer still to the German *Haus* or the French *maison*. The basic unit of traditional social organization in Japan, the *ie* is a corporate body which owns household property, carries on a family business, and emphasizes the continuity of the family line and family business over generations. This institution became established among the aristocratic and warrior classes a thousand years ago, and among the peasant class around the eighteenth century. Unlike the Chinese *jia*, the *ie* system is not purely patrilineal, since the headship may be inherited by an adopted son or son-in-law—a feature which is considered characteristic of the Japanese *ie*.

In the terminology of family systems, the *ie* consists of a stem family, that is, only one of the children continues to live with the parents after marriage. In this respect it differs from the nuclear family system, seen for example in Britain and the United States, where all of the children set up independent households, and also from the joint family system typically seen in China and India, where all male children continue to live with their parents after marriage. In the *ie*, the one child who remains in the parental home (preferably a son, if there is one) succeeds to the headship of the corporate body. The typical *ie* system is today seen chiefly among farmers and practitioners of traditional arts and crafts.

At the opposite pole of the postwar history of the family is the nuclear family. This was originally a technical term used by social anthropologists and family sociologists. In its technical sense, the nuclear family is an indivisible unit which, like an atom, can either exist alone or combine with other such units to form various types of family. As defined by the anthropologist George P. Murdock in 1949, it denotes a family unit that consists of a father, mother, and unmarried children.[1] In popular usage, however, the term is often loosely applied to what specialists would call a "nuclear family household," that is, a single nuclear family existing on its own, living apart from other kin.

When we speak of "the nuclearization of the family"—a piece of jargon from modernization theory which has become particularly well-established in Japan—we are actually referring to an increase in the number of nuclear family *households*. In technical terms, nuclearization of the family can be defined as an increase in the ratio of nuclear family households to total ordinary households. This ratio did indeed increase in Japan during the 1960s, and its rise is often said to represent a wholesale conversion of the *ie* to the nuclear family. However, this interpretation should not simply be accepted at face value.

To understand why not, we need to refer to figure 4-1. The line at the top of this graph shows the changing ratio of nuclear family households. It is noticeable that, despite all the attention paid to the nuclearization of the family at the time, the rise in this ratio during the high-growth era was not especially great. The ratio of nuclear family households was 59.6 percent in 1955, and 63.9 percent in 1975—a rise of barely 4.3 percentage points in two decades.

The bar graph in the lower part of figure 4-1, which plots actual numbers of households instead of their ratios to the total

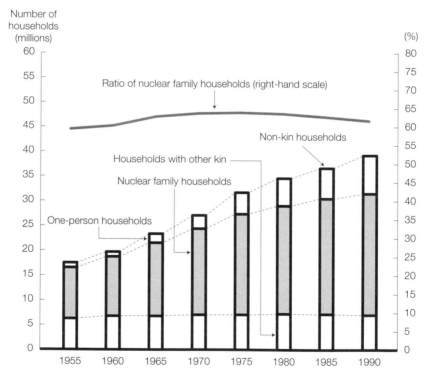

Fig. 4-1. Number of households by household type

Source: Statistics Bureau, Management and Coordination Agency, *Kokusei chosa hokoku* (National census reports).

number, reveals a hidden catch in the concept of nuclearization. True, nuclear family households have shown a steady increase, numerically as well as proportionally, from the 1960s to the present. But the graph shows another very significant fact: their rise has not been offset by a decline in the "households with other kin," which consist mainly of extended families. If the *ie* had been replaced by the nuclear family, as we are told, we would expect to see a drop in the number of extended family households. But while their *relative* weight has decreased as the total number of households has risen (due to the increase in nuclear family and single-person households), their actual numbers have remained constant.[2] In other words, nearly all of the old *ie* have had successors who continued to live with their parents after marriage, maintaining the continuity of these extended family households.

A FOND FAREWELL TO THE EXTENDED FAMILY

The term "nuclearization of the family" is thus quite misleading. It gives the impression that all of the existing *ie*, with their three generations under one roof, were fragmented during the era of high growth. But this is at odds with the facts.

There is, however, a very simple but convincing explanation for the data we have seen: in the generation in which nuclearization is said to have taken place, families contained many siblings.[3] Thus, there were many younger sons and many daughters who were free to leave their parents' household, since under the stem family system only the eldest son and his wife were expected to remain. In the postwar exodus from rural areas, large numbers of these nonsuccessor siblings created nuclear families of their own in the cities. Nuclearization progressed for demographic reasons, without posing any need to change the residential rules of the *ie* system.

The nonsuccessor siblings were secure in the knowledge that their eldest brother had stayed at home to ensure the continuity of their original family line. They also understood that if anything should happen to their brother, one of them would have to move back home. Moreover, they carried with them a vague sense that perhaps, after all, a real family was one like their brother's in the country, one which included Grandpa and Grandma together with one's own spouse and children.

The 1960s were the golden age of the television shows known as "home dramas," and the images presented by these shows give us some interesting insights into the contemporary audience's cherished notions of the family.[4] For a few years at the beginning of the sixties, sitcoms imported from America were popular. Japanese viewers are said to have been very attracted by the image these sitcoms presented, which typically featured an idealized nuclear family with an understanding father at its center, as in *Father Knows Best*.

Yet the home dramas made in Japan very soon took a different tack. The year of the Tokyo Olympics, 1964, was also a bumper year for home dramas; among the shows that debuted were *Shichinin no mago* (Seven grandchildren) and *Tadaima jui-chinin* (Right now there are eleven of us). From then on, depictions of large, three-generational families became staple home-drama fare. Another feature that dates from this time was the abundance of scenes of the family circle gathered around the meal table—prompting an alternative name for the genre, "meal-time dramas."

The mere size of the TV families does not necessarily mean that these were full-fledged *ie*. The programs of this era typically downplayed the less heartwarming aspects of the traditional system, such as the father's authority and the subservient position of the daughter-in-law. The result was big, happy families enveloped in a warm glow of mutual love. The shows had fashioned their image of the ideal family by neatly meshing two quite disparate elements: the form of the *ie* system and the content of the postwar, democratic nuclear family. The home-drama audience was able to watch this inherently flawed image without being troubled by its internal contradictions, because the audience itself was made up of people who had created nuclear families for demographic reasons, without rejecting the *ie* system in principle.

Perhaps the real secret of *Sazae-san*'s immense success lies in the ingenious device the show used to link two contradictory ideals of the family in a seamless way: that is, the fact that the young couple and their child live with Sazae's parents, rather than with her husband Masuo's. Although this has always been far less common statistically than living with the husband's parents, it was probably the only way in which the producers could portray the joys of extended-family living while leaving out the thorniest aspect of the *ie*'s traditional relationships, namely, the rivalry between the wife and her mother-in-law. (Recently, it seems, the program has even given the language a new phrase, "the Masuo-san phenomenon," referring to the trend toward co-residence with the wife's parents which appeared in the 1980s, as we will see in chapter 9.)

Although the majority of families in the 1960s were nuclear, the extended family still held a special place in their hearts, as the popularity of *Sazae-san* and the home dramas indicates. This is not to suggest that prewar attitudes had been carried over intact. The members of nuclear families liked their newfound freedom from the confines of the *ie* system. But in fact they had never been forced to make a clean break with that system. It would have taken considerable courage for an only son, or the son who was expected to inherit the household, to leave the parental home; he would have had to justify his decision, and his parents would probably have opposed it. However, very few of the people who formed nuclear families in this era would have encountered such opposition. As arrangements had already been made for one sibling to live with their parents, they were, in effect, "spares." They formed their nuclear families by chance, so to speak, and were able to enjoy a more democratic style of family living as a result, while the traditional values of the *ie* system continued to exist in the background of their lives. Thus, in my view, the 1960s were characterized by nuclearization of the family without a serious break being made with the *ie* system.

DEMOGRAPHIC GENERATIONS

Having mentioned the number of siblings as an operative factor here, we must recognize the importance, in any discussion of postwar Japanese society, of what can be called the demographic generations. Recent work indicates that their importance, though seldom noted in the past, is crucial to an understanding of both the economy and the family in postwar Japan.

Readers may be familiar with the term "demographic transition." Although detailed analyses reveal some exceptions, the theory of the demographic transition states, in general, that as modernization progresses, a society's population structure tends to change, moving from a high birthrate coupled with high infant and child mortality to a low birthrate coupled with low infant and child mortality. Present-day Japan, Europe, and the United States are societies of the latter type, where relatively few children are born but nearly all live to adulthood. In societies of both types, the number of children per couple who reach maturity will be about two. In other words, societies of both types have a stable population size. During the transition from one type to the other, however, there is often a period when a high birthrate is coupled with low infant mortality; that is to say, while people continue to have as many children as in the past, better sanitation and nutrition allow more of these children to survive. At this point, rapid population growth ensues. The decline in fertility which marks the final stage of the demographic transition is known as the fertility transition; we saw in chapter 3 how this occurred in Europe.

One hears much uninformed comment on population growth in the Third World. What the population statistics actually reflect is the fact that many societies in the Third World are currently experiencing conditions of high birthrate and low infant mortality. In the nineteenth century, it was Europe that had a population explosion, and Japan's own population has quadrupled from the stable level seen in the Tokugawa Period (1603–1867). Pre-transitional societies have always regulated their population size to maintain stability, both by design and otherwise, through an array of practices besides the natural mechanism of high fertility and high infant mortality. When a society enters the transition stage, whether one regards it as having lost its former balance or as being in the process of development, it is at this time that a population explosion occurs.

Returning now to the demographic generations in Japan: Ito Tatsuya of the Ministry of Health and Welfare's Institute of Population Problems has proposed the following demarcation into three generations: a transitional generation, born between 1925 and 1950, (that is, from just before the beginning of the Showa Period [1926–1989] to the end of the postwar baby boom); and the generations immediately before and after it, which can be called pre- and post-transitional.[5] Twenty-five years is astonishingly short for a period of demographic transition. It amounts to a single generation in the genealogical sense; thus, the three demographic generations were in fact parents, children, and grandchildren. Japan was the first society to experience the demographic transition within the space of three generations. And from this bewilderingly rapid change, a number of demographic characteristics have resulted.

THE DEMOGRAPHIC UNIQUENESS OF THE POSTWAR SYSTEM

Which of these three generations created the Postwar Family System? A person born in 1925 and marrying at age 25 would have married in 1950; one born in 1950, also marrying at age 25, would have married in 1975. The transitional generation thus married shortly after the war and was responsible for forming the majority of new families until about 1975. The dates correspond to the stable period of the Postwar Family System. This suggests that while the postwar family in Japan appeared to be following a well-trodden path of modernization (leading, for example, to the housewife role for women and a smaller number of children per couple), there were also localized demographic conditions at work.

One characteristic of the transitional generation, born during the phase of high fertility and low mortality, is their sheer numbers. The population of this cohort was about twice that of the cohort born in the preceding twenty-five years. As they aged, the population structure of Japanese society has altered (figure 4-2).

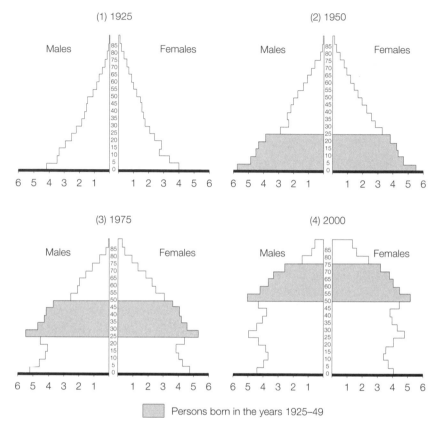

Fig. 4-2. Changes in the age structure, by gender

Sources: Ito Tatsuya, *Seikatsu no naka no jinkogaku* (Demography in everyday life) (Tokyo: Kokin Shoin, 1994), p.190. Data from Statistics Bureau, Management and Coordination Agency, *Kokusei chosa hokoku* (National census reports) and Institute of Population Problems, Ministry of Health and Welfare, *Nihon no shorai suikei jinko* (Future population projections for Japan), provisional estimates, 1991.

These demographic conditions made it possible for Japan to achieve a rate of economic growth that has seldom been paralleled. But the availability of a large work force was not, in itself, a guarantee of success. In developing his Income-Doubling Plan of 1960, Prime Minister Ikeda Hayato is said to have heeded the warning of population predictions: that without rapid economic growth, the Japanese people would face unemployment.[6]

What did this doubling of numbers from one generation to the next mean at an individual level? Simple arithmetic shows that, on average, each couple of parents must have raised four children to maturity. From the children's viewpoint, it means that even as adults they had many siblings (table 4-1).

One often hears that people in times past had many brothers and sisters. Strictly speaking, only the generation born in the years 1925–50 was characterized by having many siblings who all survived to adulthood. But the transitional generation became the mainstay of postwar Japanese society, and its members have a strong tendency to base value judgements on their own group experience. One wishes they were more aware that the demographic conditions they experienced were unique, and that those of us born later could not follow directly in their footsteps if we tried. The implications of this point will become obvious when we look at sibling networks.

Because the Postwar Family System rested on the shoulders of this transitional generation, it was shaped by various conditions unique to that generation. The consequences were, I think, twofold. First, as we saw earlier in this chapter, the nuclearization of the family was not necessarily accompanied by a break with the *ie* system. The *ie* did, of course, change considerably in nature after the war, but there was no practical need to do away with the system as a whole. At the very least, the norm of the successor's family living with his parents under the stem family system did not die out.

Table 4-1. Changes in relative cohort size, 1925–2025

Cohorts ratios	1925	1950	1975	2000	2025
ages 25–49 / ages 50–74	2.17	2.17	2.12	1.09	0.88
ages 0–24 / ages 25–49	1.84	1.83	1.00	0.81	0.94
ages 50–74 / ages 25–49	0.46	0.46	0.47	0.91	1.14

Sources: Economic Planning Agency, *Kokumin seikatsu hakusho Heisei 6 nendoban* (White paper on the national life, fiscal 1994), Table 1-2-22. Data from Statistics Bureau, Management and Coordination Agency, *Kokusei chosa hokoku* (National census reports), and Institute of Population Problems, Ministry of Health and Welfare, *Nihon no shorai suikei jinko* (Future population projections for Japan), estimates as of September 1992.

According to a study by Hiroshima Kiyoshi using demographic models, the norm of the stem family system has in fact weakened since the era of high economic growth. Until 1955 the prevalence of parent-child co-residence from the time of the child's marriage stood at about 90 percent, but by 1975 it had fallen to 37.5 percent. At the same time, however, there was a growing trend toward co-residence beginning some time after the child's marriage; hence, it can be said that the stem family norm has survived in a changing form.[7]

In the era of the Postwar Family System, the shift from the *ie* to the nuclear family had begun. But because it was the second demographic generation that was carrying it out, the speed of this change remained slower than the increase in the number of nuclear families would seem to suggest. Demographic conditions were acting to cushion social change.

SIBLING NETWORKS

The second consequence of the transitional generation's major role in supporting the Postwar Family System was that families had ready-made social networks.

As we saw in chapter 2, in the 1960s the residents of the suburban housing complexes known as *danchi* were in the vanguard of a new lifestyle. Because such apartment complexes were still a rarity, *danchi* life was the subject of many surveys, and one of the findings was that the residents had little contact with their neighbors.

Although it is sometimes claimed that urban living does not allow the development of communities, the contrary was found to be true in studies done in the United States by urban sociologists of the Chicago School. William Whyte reported that in the suburban housing areas he studied, ". . . not even the apartment is a redoubt; people don't bother to knock and they come and go furiously."[8] Nevertheless, the reports that residents of suburban housing complexes in postwar Japan did not associate freely with their neighbors were evidently true. In 1960, Masuda Kokichi wrote: "Studies conducted to date with regard to [*danchi*-type] apartment buildings in Japan's suburbs have all reported a low level of neighbor interaction, whether among heads of household or housewives."[9]

The reason for this was much debated at the time. Cultural factors considered to be specific to Japan, such as a low level of public consciousness or the familism of the Japanese, were often called on to explain the findings. Moreover, in the lingering aftermath of the national loss of confidence which had followed defeat in the war, the explanations seem to have been framed largely in negative terms.

Interestingly enough, by the end of the 1970s the same lack of neighborly contact was being hailed as a sign of "Japanese-style welfare." According to this rationale, families in Japan were so self-reliant that they never needed help from their neighbors, nor from public services, hence there was no need for social welfare institutions—or there would be no need, if only families were as solid as they had been in the sixties. What was really meant here by "families" was housewives. Put bluntly, the argument ran: We wouldn't have a social welfare problem if housewives did their job. If they tried harder, they could take proper care of their children and the elderly, too. Japan is expected to become an aged society, so you housewives had better get your act together.

Not finding this argument very persuasive myself, I took a closer look at the data in the original social surveys, and was struck by something which the survey-takers had most likely taken for granted: the existence of kin networks.

When studies published in the 1960s dealt with kin networks, the emphasis was on their perceived weakness. People no longer saw as much of their uncles, aunts, and cousins as they had in the past, but associated solely with the members of their particular family of origin, that is, their parents and siblings. One writer pointed out that "a quite limited scope of interaction with relatives, extending only as far as parents and siblings, is a characteristic of newly founded households."[10] The networks that existed in the 1960s probably did appear very meager by comparison with the formalized kinship organizations that had traditionally existed under the *ie* system. These reached beyond the family of origin to include relationships among the original and branch households, and corporate groups of kin composed of a set of households usually residing in the same area. But from the perspective of the 1990s, the kin networks of the sixties begin to look quite robust.

For example, take the availability of help from relatives in looking after young children. A survey which I conducted in 1986 found that mothers in Hyogo Prefecture received little or no help from their siblings; they could still rely on their parents, but that was as far as their kin networks extended. This is in stark contrast with the wide-ranging support which the many siblings of the demographic second generation gave one another, even after they had moved to the cities. Sisters visited one another frequently, especially while their children were small, and the cousins who were brought together in this way often grew up as close as brothers and sisters.

In a 1965 survey conducted by Morioka Kiyomi et al. in the Hibarigaoka housing development in Tokyo, married women in an age group in which the majority had small children were asked how many times they saw various relatives per month. The frequency of contact with each relative was expressed as the percentage of women in the sample who reported making or receiving at least one visit per month. The women reported seeing the following relatives, in decreasing order of frequency: own parents (37 percent), husband's parents (31 percent), own siblings (29 percent), husband's siblings (16 percent). The relative importance of the wife's siblings, ranking close behind the two sets of parents, is impressive.[11]

The studies cited in 1960 by Masuda showed that those housewives who had little contact with their neighbors were in close contact with their relatives, while those housewives who saw little of their relatives did in fact associate quite actively with their neighbors (table 4-2).[12] Neighborhood networks replaced kin networks, and vice versa. The two types of network were also found to be interchangeable in the 1980s. But in the 1960s there was little need to turn to the neighbors as strong kin networks—in practice, sibling networks—were still in place. This is a very dif-

Table 4-2. Number of visits to parents made by housewives with different attitudes to neighbor interaction

No. of visits per year	0	1–2	3–4	5–	Unknown	
Attitude to neighbor interaction						
Positive	20.1	45.5	6.0	27.3	1.1	100.0%
Neutral or indifferent	10.0	45.1	15.3	27.7	1.8	100.0
Negative	8.9	41.5	7.3	40.5	1.8	100.0

Source: From Masuda Kokichi, "Neighbor interaction among resident families in *danchi*-type apartment buildings."[9]

ferent conclusion from the one reached by proponents of "Japanese-style welfare," namely, that families in the sixties were able to live with no social networks at all.[13]

Let me summarize here what we have been discussing. In comparison with the social relationships of families today, those of the 1960s were characterized by stronger kin networks, as a result of the fact that the transitional generation had many siblings. Thus, the ability of families in the sixties to care for their infant children and elderly members without seeking help from neighborhood networks or public institutions was not a sign of greater strength or effort on their part, but was, in fact, made possible by the support of their relatives.

Indeed, there has probably never been a time, in Japan or any society, when families have raised their children and taken care of elderly members without outside help. Even in the modernizing Meiji Period (1868–1912), there were always large numbers of people who interacted with a growing child, including various kinds of fictive parents (such as godparents); the masters and mistresses in whose homes young people were placed as domestic servants; and peer groups in the traditional young men's and young women's lodges in rural communities. The makeup of the support networks may have changed over time, but it is almost inconceivable that they could vanish altogether.

The notion that the family would assume sole responsibility for every important aspect of human life, from cradle to grave, is of fairly recent origin. Most likely it developed in conjunction with the rise of the modern family, which we will examine in the next chapter. Nevertheless, in the West, the modern family, contrary to its defining principles of exclusiveness and privacy, drew on quite extensive neighborhood networks. And although urban Japanese families in the 1960s appeared to lack any outside assistance, in practice they were quietly drawing on the help of the kin networks that demographic conditions had made available.

Once we recognize that it was the demographic transitional generation which supported the Postwar Family System, it becomes clear that demographics can account for many observed facts—such as the residual consciousness of the *ie*, or the family's high degree of self-reliance—which were formerly attributed to uniquely Japanese cultural factors. While culture is undoubtedly important, I do not hold with the method of argument which is quick to reach for vague cultural generalizations when other, more specific causes are at hand. In this connection, the importance of the demographic generations in discussing postwar Japan cannot be overemphasized.

| # The Postwar Family System

THE POSTWAR SYSTEM AND THE FAMILY

In the previous chapter we began to apply the newly coined term "Postwar Family System" to the period during which the postwar family in its most typical form remained stable. We have seen the features which typified this family in chapters 1 to 4. We looked briefly at how they were reflected in two TV series; since *Sazae-san* is atypical in some ways, it would be best to picture the family in *Chibi Maruko-chan*: Mother is a housewife, there are two children, and three generations live together, (which was the aspiration, although in practice nuclear family households were more common).

Postwar changes in the family, it seems, have generally been assumed to be incremental and unidirectional. The idea of a progression from the *ie* to the nuclear family is one example, and the belief that the family has gradually malfunctioned is another. The misconceptions that women's participation in society has steadily increased since the war, and that the birthrate has steadily fallen until it eventually dropped below the replacement level, can probably also be traced to an unexamined assumption of unidirectional change.

However, on looking with an open mind at statistics such as the female labor force participation rate and the birthrate, one soon discovers that they cannot be read in this way. The bottom of the M-shaped curve first dropped, then rebounded. The graph of the birthrate also shows distinctly the existence of a stable interval. Clearly, aspects of society related to the family took on a stable structure at a certain point after the war. The postwar years can thus be divided into the period before this structure was completed; the period of its stability; and the period during which it disintegrated. This way of looking at the evidence seems to me to be far more appropriate than a unidirectional model.

In an economic or political context, the terms "postwar system" or "postwar structure" immediately bring to mind certain distinctive features. In Japanese politics we speak of the "1955 system." That year saw both the merger of conservative parties to form the Liberal Democratic Party (LDP) and the unification of the Japan Socialist Party (JSP). In the power structure thus established, the LDP held a stable position of dominance, with the JSP heading a number of smaller and weaker parties in opposition. Economically, we associate the postwar period with rapid growth. Japan's postwar system is thus practically synonymous with a high rate of growth under stable LDP rule. To this we may add, in the arena of foreign relations, the bipolar Cold War structure and the U.S.-Japan security treaties.

From a worldwide perspective, the international wave of student protest and the first energy crisis marked the beginning of a reshaping of the postwar structure in the 1970s. Japan's booming economy continued to thrive even after the oil crises hit Western nations hard. By the early 1990s, however, after witnessing the fall of the Berlin wall and, at home, the bursting of the economic bubble and the breakup of the LDP, the Japanese too were becoming keenly aware that the postwar system had ended.

In general, our understanding of postwar history is already shaped by a framework of this kind. Yet little attempt has been made to situate the family within the same framework. One suspects that this is because changes in the family, or relationships between women and men, have been consigned to the private sphere.

The public and the private have long been regarded as separate realms. Sociohistorical change has been viewed as consisting exclusively of those changes which belong to the public sphere, and social and historical eras have been defined accordingly. In comparison, until recently, changes in the family have received less serious attention.

In discussing the origins of housework, I stressed that domestic labor was not always separated from other forms of labor. The dividing line was drawn at a certain point in history, during the process of modernization. Thus the separation of the public and private spheres was itself an historical event. Once we realize this, the idea that history consists only of changes in the public domain is revealed as a construct of modern society. Not only are both the public and the private spheres part of "society"; so, too, is the very distinction between them. For a long time, the family and the relationship between the sexes were regarded as entirely separate from politics and economics, but this has never been so.

THE BIRTH OF THE MODERN FAMILY

What, then, were the characteristics of the Postwar Family System? The points we have discussed so far can be organized under three headings: (1) the shift to the housewife role for women, (2) reproductive egalitarianism, and (3) the effects of demographic transition.

The first two of these characteristics were not unique to Japan. I have referred several times to the existence of a field known as the social history of the family. The results of work done in this field in other countries overlap with points (1) and (2) to a considerable extent. We have already seen that the housewife's origins date from the modern era in Western countries also; for example, we noted the research done on the development of the housewife's role in Germany, and the influence of Mrs. Beeton's *Book of Household Management* in Britain. And with regard to point (2), drawing on the work of Ariès and others, we have recognized as widespread modern phenomena the foregrounding of love toward children, the exaltation of mother love, and the establishment of motherhood as women's primary role. The experience of postwar Japan, with full-time housewives becoming a majority, couples having fewer children, and the mother's love weighing heavily on those children, was common to European and North American societies. In view of this, perhaps it is time we paused to reevaluate Japan's Postwar Family System in the context of world history.

Social historians of the family have introduced an important concept: the modern family.[1] In postwar Japan, in general usage a "modern" family has been taken to mean a democratic family. One of the leaders of the intellectual democratization movement that arose after the war was Kawashima Takeyoshi, a scholar of family law whose seminal book *Nihon shakai no kazokuteki kosei* (The familial structure of Japanese society), published in 1948, could be called the starting point of postwar family theory in Japan. In the introduction, Kawashima wrote: "The greatest task presently facing the Japanese people is, needless to say, the democratization of our nation . . . . The democratic revolution cannot overlook the family system, once an object of absolute faith for the Japanese race, nor can democracy be achieved if the family system is overlooked."[2]

The expressions "modern-style family" and "democratic family"—representing not so much a reality as an ideal yet to be realized—continued to be used for many years as stock phrases in discussing the family. They embodied the concept of a transition from the feudalistic, patriarchal *ie* that had existed under the 1898 Civil Code to the modern-style democratic family envisioned in the 1948 Civil Code. This transition also implied replacing the *ie*, which was specific to Japanese culture, with an ideal universal family, as represented by the nuclear family of the United States and Europe.

However, there were significant differences between this modern-style family and the concept of the modern family developed by social historians, although both refer to essentially the same entity. Social historians have seldom defined the term "modern family" precisely, but one learns from their writings that they ascribe to it more or less the following characteristics:[3]

1. Separation of the domestic and public spheres
2. Strong emotional relationships among family members
3. The centrality of children
4. A gender-based division of labor, with the public sphere assigned to men and the domestic sphere to women

5. A strengthening of the group solidarity of the family
6. A decline of social interaction and *sociabilité*, and the establishment of privacy
7. Exclusion of non-relatives
(8. Existence as a nuclear family household)

I believe it is better to enclose point (8) in parentheses when discussing a society such as Japan which continues to form extended families, since a household may include grandparents and yet qualify as a modern family on every other count.

THE PITFALLS OF FAMILY THEORY

Interestingly, and perhaps ironically, people are not conscious of the special characteristics which shape the era in which they live; they take them for granted, seeing them simply as the human condition. What is truly important becomes visible only with hindsight.

Thus, the above list of characteristics of the modern family might well prompt the surprised response, "But what other kind of family is there?" When I ask my college classes "What is a family?" the replies I receive most often fall into the area of (2), emotional relationships. The students speak of families, in general, as people with whom one can be open, feel relaxed, and talk about anything, and as people who love each other. Indeed, all the items from (1) to (8) could be taken to be rather obvious attributes of families in general, hardly requiring the label "modern."

Indeed, the definition of the family conventionally used in family sociology bears a close resemblance to the above list. For comparison, here is a list of postulations and background assumptions[4] regarding the family, compiled from three representative textbooks of family sociology used in the United States and Japan, namely, *The Family* by Waller and Hill (1938, 1951), *A Modern Introduction to the Family* by Bell and Vogel (1960), and *Atarashii kazoku shakaigaku* (New family sociology) by Morioka and Mochizuki (1983):[5]

a. The family exists universally in human society.
b. The family has an essential nature which does not change

under different historical and cultural conditions.

c. The family is a group.
d. The family is composed mainly of kin.
e. Family members are bound by strong emotional ties.
f. The most basic function of the family is the socialization of children.
g. Family members have different roles according to gender.
h. The basic type of family is the nuclear family.

Points (c) to (h) closely resemble characteristics listed for the modern family, while points (a) and (b) assert that families with such characteristics are common to every society. Why, then, apply the label "the modern family" when, in effect, these same items appear to constitute a universal definition of the family?

In fact, social historians introduced the term "modern family" in order to contest this very point. Despite the claims of family sociology textbooks, the family these texts describe has not been universal throughout history. It is a purely historical phenomenon, one that came into being at a certain point in time. Thus, the study of the social history of the family has not only brought to light the nature of families in the past, but has led to a bold proposal to overturn the definition of the family long accepted by the academic world.

It seems to have been family researchers in twentieth-century America who were chiefly responsible for mistaking the features of the modern family for universal truths. In nineteenth-century Europe, the prevalent view of the family was influenced by the theory of evolution, and scholars were well aware that different types of family existed. But in twentieth-century America, particularly after World War II, the conviction grew that the family as it existed in that society was the universal type. The anthropologist George P. Murdock, in his book *Social Structure* (1949), asserted that the nuclear family was the universal basic unit of the family, found in every human society. Murdock's work had a great impact on sociologists such as Talcott Parsons, and can probably be called the most influential family theory of the twentieth century.[6]

In the wake of defeat in World War II, Japan had no choice but to accept this framework unreservedly. What it promised was a transition from the *ie* system which was specific to Japan, to the nuclear family which was universal to humankind. The nuclear or modern-style family—for these are very nearly synonymous—was not only seen as desirable in terms of values, but also acquired theoretical legitimacy as the true form of the family which would inevitably emerge if external constraints were removed.[7]

Sooner or later, however, such a theoretical framework is bound to be pushed to its limits. Having universalized the particular form at which one has arrived, namely, the modern family, one is left with no way to interpret any further changes beyond that form. Thus, when the form of the family which is supposedly universal to humankind begins to show signs of changing, one has a major crisis on one's hands. As early as the first half of the 1960s, sociologist Yamamuro Shuhei expressed concern over the idealization of the nuclear family, which he saw as "enforc[ing] a single idealized image." With remarkable perceptiveness, Yamamuro warned: "We cannot entirely rule out the danger that this idealization may become an obstacle to solving" the family "crisis" that followed modernization.[8]

Today, precisely because the family is in a state of flux, we have come to realize that what was once thought to be an immutable ideal was actually just one of many possible configurations, namely, the historical entity we now know as the modern family. In formulating this concept, perhaps the greatest service that social historians performed was to teach us that what had come to be taken for granted as "the family" could not be taken for granted, and, further, that it did not signal the end of the world just because the family was changing, women were going out to work, or families without children were on the increase.

THE TWENTIETH-CENTURY MODERN FAMILY

There is one last matter to consider: Is the modern family a single entity, or has it varied over time or in different cultures?

Historically, the modern family is thought to have become established from the mid-eighteenth to the nineteenth century. Historical research has tended to focus mainly on the nineteenth century as the golden age of the modern family. But since, as we will discover, there were substantial differences between the nine-teenth- and twentieth-century versions of the modern family, we should distinguish between these two rather than view the nine-teenth-century modern family as an enduring type.

One distinguishing feature was that it was not until the twenti-eth century that the modern family became a mass phenomenon. In the 1800s, modern families were found only in the middle class. As we saw earlier, they had domestic servants. But the families of the servants themselves could not have been characterized as modern.

During the late eighteenth and early nineteenth centuries, when the modern family was becoming established among the European middle classes, working-class families had a very differ-ent visage. Although the images we have of drunken children and brawling couples in the poorer strata of European society have come to us through the disapproving eyes of the middle class, it does seem that, at the very least, the families of workers did not fit the modern family ideal of loving emotional bonds, gracious women, and innocent children. And the members of the working class, it should be noted, saw nothing wrong with this state of affairs. In the eyes of the middle class, working-class families appeared to have broken down; strictly speaking, however, the family as the middle class knew it had yet to be established in the working class.

During the nineteenth century, educational campaigns by the middle class and a desire for self-betterment led to changes among workers' families. From mid-century onward, working-class mothers who could not tend their children full-time began to feel dissatisfied. There was a gradual shift, starting with those house-holds which could afford it, to the full-time housewife's role for working men's wives. But it was not until the twentieth century that this shift to the modern family as mass phenomenon reached completion in Europe, in the years between the two world wars.

These were also the years in which Europe saw dramatic demographic changes. In chapter 3, we looked briefly at a key ele-ment in the history of the family in Northwestern Europe, the European marriage pattern. During the period from about 1930 to

1940, this pattern of late and less-than-universal marriage gave way to early and universal marriage, while at the same time the steep decline in marital fertility which had continued since the 1870s hit bottom. It became standard to marry and form a family of two or three cherished children. In chapter 3 I called this standardization "reproductive egalitarianism," and these egalitarian trends can be interpreted as statistical signs that the modern family had become a mass phenomenon extending to every class. It also appears that Europe's female labor force participation rates had declined at that time. This is yet another statistical sign of the popularization of the modern family.

Clearly, then, it was not until the twentieth century that the modern family became universally established in Europe (and in the United States). Modern families had existed before then, but as just one of various family types which existed simultaneously. Although the modern family was held to be more ideal than the other types, it had not yet supplanted them entirely; people in the nineteenth century still accepted that others lived differently. It was only in the twentieth century that the ideal of the modern family became all-pervasive.

When we thus distinguish the twentieth-century modern family from that of the nineteenth century, it becomes clear that the concept of the family utilized in the social sciences was predicated on the twentieth-century modern family. When speaking of "the family" in these fields, it was conventionally assumed that the housework was done by the housewife, not by servants; nor were there usually assumed to be eight or ten children. Above all, it was taken for granted that the same family type was found in all social strata. Thus, what both laypeople and social scientists have tacitly understood to be "the family" has in fact been the twentieth-century modern family. Social historians studying the modern family have tended till now to focus on its nineteenth-century form, but in view of this implicit equation with "the family," perhaps more scholarly attention should be directed in the future toward the twentieth-century form.

On further reflection, we can see that the Postwar Family System represented the establishment of the twentieth-century modern family in Japan. During the Taisho Period (1912–1926), Japan was, in effect, passing through that phase of the modern family's development which occurred in the West during the nineteenth century. The Taisho Period modern family did not exist in every stratum of society but was limited to the urban middle class, who had domestic servants. In Japan, the transition to a mass phenomenon, or what we might call the twentieth-century modern family proper, took place after World War II.

It is worth noting, in passing, that a number of other trends in postwar Japan (especially during the high-growth era) dated back, in the West, to the years between the two world wars. In Japan the words "prewar" and "postwar" tend to be associated solely with World War II. In the West, however, currents which first emerged after World War I took on a fully realized form after World War II. For example, both the Russian Revolution and the rise of American power date from around the end of World War I; the resulting geopolitical structure merely reached completion in the post-World War II era.

WAS THE POSTWAR FAMILY IN JAPAN UNIQUE IN ANY WAY?

We might well ask at this point whether the postwar family in Japan was simply one example of a worldwide trend of modernization, having all of its features in common with other nations, or were there some characteristics that were specifically Japanese? An argument could probably be made to show, for example, that something resembling the modern family became established in postwar Japan, but that because of the continuing influence of the *ie* mentality and familism it should be referred to in a culturally specific way, say, "the Japanese-style modern family." However, I do not intend to present such an argument. While the importance of culture is undeniable, unless we ask how cultural continuities came into being we will merely be resorting to "culture" as an all-explanatory magic term, an excuse for not pursuing our theoretical inquiry further.

This is where the third characteristic of the Postwar Family System, namely, the effects of demographic transition, comes in. Because the late 1950s, when the Postwar Family System was established, were also the years when the demographic transition was reaching completion, many aspects become clearer in the light of demographic considerations, and yet, for some reason, these have tended to be overlooked. The Postwar Family System did indeed differ in certain respects from the twentieth-century modern family in Western nations. Japanese families continued to cherish the ideal of three generations living together even as, in practice, the shift toward two-generational nuclear families progressed; they withdrew into a shell of home- and family-centered life and had comparatively little contact with the surrounding community; and they also attempted to take on the full burden of caring for children and the elderly within the family, apparently with considerable success. But cultural factors alone are not sufficient to explain each of these aspects; we must also look at demographic factors. The existence of a stem family system in which the successor lives with his parents is, of course, a cultural factor, but it was demographic conditions that made it possible for this system to continue in the midst of the nuclearization of the family.

Moreover, the demographic conditions involved are those which are quite generally found accompanying modernization, namely, the changes that occur in the demographic transition. If we were determined to find some aspect unique to Japan, we could perhaps say that the speed of these changes was demographically unique.

It is time we moved away from the method of interpreting social phenomena whereby the experience of Western nations gives rise to general laws, and anything not covered by these laws becomes culture-specific. Many of the observed differences between regions or periods can be explained in terms of different combinations or rates of progress of quite general phenomena. And cultures themselves, being in a continuous relationship with other changing factors, also change with time.

Chapter 6 | Women's Liberation and the Dissolution of the Family

WHAT WAS "WOMEN'S LIB" IN JAPAN?

In previous chapters, we discussed the formation of the Postwar Family System and looked at its three defining characteristics. But this part of the story is now ancient history, for we are already two decades into the next era. In this chapter we will begin to ask what has become of this system and where we in Japan find ourselves now—in other words, to address topics which are more directly relevant to contemporary life.

As we saw in figures 1-2, 3-1, and 4-1, changes in statistical indices of the family started to show up around 1975. The events which will concern us in this chapter date back a few years further, however. While it is unusual for developments in the family to make their appearance in the form of social incidents or a social movement, this was exactly what happened in the early seventies. I am referring to the movement known in Japan as *uman ribu*.

Uman ribu is a transliteration of the English "women's lib." Initially used in a derogatory sense, it was quickly adopted by members of the Japanese movement themselves, although there was already a neutral and more formal term for women's liberation, *josei kaiho*. In claiming the new title for themselves, they sought to embrace the negative image and turn it into a positive expression of their own identity. I will follow their usage here and refer to the Japanese movement as "women's lib." However, it should be added that—unlike the English term, which may sound dated today but is not specific to one era—"women's lib" in Japan denotes the women's movement as it was in the early seventies, as distinct from the *feminizumu* (feminism) which emerged in the mid-seventies.

Before we look at its implications for change in the family, we need to examine the substance of the movement in Japan. For the public perception of Japanese women's lib was surprisingly inaccurate at the time, and remains so to this day.

WHAT WOMEN'S LIB MEANT TO ME

Let me first make my own perspective clear. In the early seventies, when the movement began, I was still in junior high school. I learned of women's demonstrations and meetings through newspapers and television, (as I also watched on live TV when the riot police turned their water cannons on student radicals occupying Tokyo University's Yasuda Hall). Thus, my earliest "experience" of women's lib was through the media.

The attitude of the contemporary media was blatantly biased. Women's lib was simply not treated as a serious social movement. An all-woman demonstration would be covered under jeering headlines such as "Red Ranting." (In Japan the color red is traditionally associated with women, and thus this gibe had nothing to do with politics.) The focus of media interest would quickly become sexual, as in reports that women at rallies in America were burning their bras. The media treated the movement as a sensational cultural fad, instead of asking what the women taking part had to say. Even now, the press has not entirely overcome its tendency to confine articles on women's issues to the "domestic section" (as the women's page is called in Japan), but the contemporary coverage of women's lib was so biased that today's newspaper editors would certainly blue-pencil it.

Not to be outdone, the mass-circulation weekly magazines featured such stories as "The Sexual Attitudes of Female Firebrands As Seen in *Onna Eros* (Woman/Eros) [a feminist magazine]," "Women on Top: Lib Luminary Touts Self-Defense against Rape and Pregnancy," and "The Cute Side of the Hothead Women Who Rush to Rallies." The media thus employed familiar male tactics to discredit the women's movement. They automatically saw the movement in terms of sex, did not take it seriously, and accused its members of being unfeminine.[1] As one activist put it at the time, the prevailing caricature suggested that "women who carry on about liberation and sex discrimination are dowdy, dried-up old maids venting their frustration."[2]

In my early teens, I would pore over such articles in the magazines my father brought home. Somehow, despite the tone of the reports, the news that there were women doing these things was very exciting to me. I felt as though I had gotten the message through all the distortions. Even as a child, every time I was told "You mustn't do that because you're a girl," I had wanted to know why. Now, as I read these articles, the fog of lingering doubts suddenly cleared. I started to realize that I wasn't the only one who felt like this, and that these feelings could be expressed in this way. I can assure anyone who thinks women's lib never amounted to more than a few highly visible women that they are wrong. Even if we couldn't be present at marches and rallies, there were many who experienced the movement as I did.

Given the bias of the reporting, however, I felt a need to find out what the women were really saying. It was only when I reached college, in 1976, that I finally came a little closer to the truth. By that time the movement which had sprung up around 1970 and reached its peak in 1972 was already on the wane. The student movement was also showing signs of terminal decline as rival New Left factions turned violently on each other, while some former activists retreated into communes. Nevertheless, I learned much about the developments in women's lib from those who had been involved, and became a voracious reader of movement pamphlets, newsletters, and magazines such as *Onna Eros*. I also helped form a small consciousness-raising group, and was active in the campaign against restriction of the grounds for legal abortion to exclude economic reasons. Thus, I was on the scene as the women's movement took on an increasingly formalized structure in the process of becoming a large-scale movement focused on specific political issues.

I have made these personal disclosures because as I talk about women's lib I want my position, and the extent to which I am entitled to speak, to be clear. A social movement is seen very differently depending on whether or not the observer was part of it. Even the individuals within a movement will see it differently according to their different standpoints as members. Perhaps my own position vis-à-vis women's lib can best be described as follows: although I was not directly involved in it myself, I felt an affinity for women's lib; however, I also experienced the changes that occurred over time as the women's movement explored new directions, when simply restating the positions taken by women's lib could no longer provide a way forward.

Until quite recently, very little had been written on Japanese women's lib. In the early 1990s, several magazines produced special features to coincide with the twentieth anniversary of the movement. A truly epoch-making event was the publication of the *Shiryo nihon uman ribu shi* (History of Japanese women's lib in documents) from 1992 to 1995.[3] By turning to this comprehensive collection of valuable primary sources, including flyers and pamphlets, we can re-create something of the spirit of the times as we trace the movement from its early stages. While quoting mainly from these volumes, I would like to review the course of women's lib and look more closely at what its members were advocating.

TRUE TO OUR WOMAN-SELVES

Women's lib first became a visible movement in Japan in 1970. At the time, the student movement and anti-Establishment protests were at their height. Following China's Cultural Revolution and the May Movement of 1968 in France, the events often referred to as the youth revolt or student rebellion were sweeping the industrialized world. This was not simply a political movement: it was accompanied by the rise of a counterculture which, with its rock music and hippie lifestyle, rejected the dominant culture's values and shook society as a whole. Women's lib emerged in part from this student movement, but at the same time was a reaction against it.

> During the campaign against the U.S.–Japan Security Treaty and the campus protests which rocked the nation in 1969, where were the women? Either they brought up the rear—forming defence commit-

tees, organizing provisions, carrying stones, etc. In other words, they kept the home fires burning. Or they were on the front lines—agitating in male language, wielding wooden staves, etc. In other words, they acted as men.[4]

Women in the struggle can be divided into the "cutie" type and the "Gewalt Rosa" type. What does the struggle mean to women?[5]

Although women and men in the student movement were fighting the same battles, it turns out that they were not sharing the same roles. Men threw stones and decided policy while (apart from a few exceptions who received special treatment as equals to men) the women made rice balls, took minutes, and often made themselves available as sexual partners.

Human being, human being, human being: this is the phrase we have used continually in the struggle. . . . Just what have we been losing by using this noun of neuter gender? Human being = male. Women have been swept away in the vortex of a world based solely on male values. . . . Men have called this the limited nature of women. But we have no such limitations, and our struggle can only begin with our becoming true to our woman-selves, true to our own sex which is different in nature from the male.[6]

Thus, one of the roots of women's liberation in Japan was the disillusionment of women student activists, who broke away from the men to start groups of their own. The New Left was hardly unique in excluding women from the category "human being," but it was in the New Left that women activists came up against this problem which is fundamental to every woman's existence.

It is worth noting that, as the phrase "becoming true to our woman-selves" suggests, from the outset women's lib was never a movement of would-be men. In this regard it has been greatly misunderstood. The motive force was an attempt by women at self-affirmation. Women who until then had been permitted only two options—to exist for men, or to receive special treatment as honorary men—decided that they wanted just to be women, and furthermore, that just being women was fine. Far from wanting to be men, they set out to find a wholly female identity, and to investigate theoretically what this meant. As they sought to objectify and strip away the conventional ways of thinking, or "male logic," in which women themselves were steeped, they often used the term "women's logic" as a kind of watchword.[7]

THERE IS NO SUCH THING AS A PRIVATE PROBLEM

What issues were being raised by the use of such expressions as "women's logic" and "true to our woman-selves"? The author of the latter phrase writes, in the same piece:

> For men, the inner and outer worlds fit together in a clear [dichotomous] structure. Thus, even in the midst of political struggle, they can continue without shame or hesitation to behave according to the rules of the old system where women are concerned, since this belongs to the private sphere. . . . For us women, however, alienation is the order of the day. It is smeared thickly all over our lives, from meals to bed, until real life consists of nothing but alienation.[8]

Women's lib set its sights on exactly this private sphere—the sphere of love, sex, and housework—which previous political movements had disregarded as they deliberated matters of state using elaborate theoretical apparatuses. More precisely, what women did was challenge the social conventions which distinguished the public from the private sphere and valued one over the other.

> There is no such thing as a private problem. We will state this categorically.[9]

The American women's liberation movement gave rise to the slogan "The personal is political." In modern society it had always been accepted that personal matters belonged to a private realm, unrelated to power and politics. But women's liberation charged that issues of power were intimately involved in personal relationships and in relations between the sexes.

To Men

Why are cooking, washing, sewing
women's work?
Can you tell me that, dear?

I like a good meal
I like to put on clean clothes
A torn seam ought to be mended

But having to have dinner ready every day
when you get home is a pain. . . .

The pain of having to do what I don't want to do is the pain of a
slave
A woman is supposed to be a free person, like you.[10]

It should be added that women's lib did address issues other than so-called "private" problems. In movement writings, one meets with a certain amount of leftist terminology which today looks decidedly stilted, and with theoretical discussions of the state and capitalism. But what was unique about this movement was the fact that, no matter what question its members discussed, they approached it in relation to sex and childbirth, women's roles, and women's concerns. Thus, when they discussed labor, their primary focus was on maternity leave and other aspects of the protection of women's reproductive health; or when they discussed Asia, the focus was on issues such as sex tours and the "comfort women" who were forced to serve in Japanese army brothels during the war.

SEX AND ABORTION

The coerciveness of unequal power relations is present even in sex. Moreover, the male-female dynamics of power revolving around sexuality are not simply personal dynamics: they are embedded in the sexual mores common to society as a whole.

I'm afraid to walk alone at night. . . . As a means of protecting myself, it might be good to learn some form of self-defence. . . . But that does nothing to change the fact that I am a target of attack. The problem lies in the fact that women are the object of rape. . . . There can be no individual solution.[11]

Sexuality, regarded as the core of private life, became the central theme of women's lib. Some writers recounted experiences which might appear entirely personal: for instance, a woman might tell of a failure of contraception, an abortion, another failure, an unwanted baby. Yet, far from being solely personal problems, the anxiety and fear brought on by pregnancy being a constant companion of sex are a concern widely shared by women.

You go to bed with him for "love," because he wants it, because he won't like you if you don't. But if you're just going to close your eyes and endure it—you couldn't care less, you wish he'd hurry up and get it over with—well, there's really no point. What a drag. You with the cold feet—a terror of getting pregnant, nightmares about VD— it's time to arm yourself with scientific knowledge and liberate yourself.[12]

Frequent references to sex provided the mass media with choice material and fueled the movement's scandalous reputation. Contrary to the popular image, however, women's lib was not necessarily extolling free sex.

"Free sex" is merely a hip way of expressing the male attitude that women can be treated like toilets, without regard for consequences. What we intend by sexual liberation is not liberation of this *Heibon Panchi* [tabloid magazine] type.
What it is, for a start, is liberation from being toilets.[13]

To me, communication means tenderness, and sex is the physical expression of this tenderness.[14]

In light of these concerns it was both highly symbolic and entirely natural that women's lib reached its peak as a movement with the 1972 campaign to prevent revision of the Eugenic Protection Law. Since this law had been enacted out of a need to limit the population, as discussed in chapter 3, in postwar Japan a pregnancy could be legally terminated for economic as well as health reasons. In the early seventies, however, there were moves to restrict the grounds for legal abortion; proponents of the revision cited the decline in the birthrate, and also spoke from the viewpoint of respect for life. A nationwide campaign against the revision was immediately organized by women, and the proposed bill was defeated in the Diet in 1974. The women's movement, which until this time had been widely dispersed in small local groups,[15] now entered a new phase.

Ironically, perhaps, for those who had been so active in the early seventies, by the time International Women's Year (1975) finally induced the media and the public to begin paying serious attention to women's issues, the main impetus of the women's movement had shifted to a new type of "post-women's lib" activism, typified by the International Women's Year Action Group. From seeking changes in women's consciousness, the emphasis moved to pressing for changes in specific legal and social institutions.

CONTESTING STEREOTYPIC IMAGES OF WOMEN

At this point in our survey of the concerns of women's lib, let us return to the central subject of this book, "the family." I have already noted that women's lib originated in part from the student movement, but this does not mean that only young, single women were involved—there were also a fair number of housewives and women with children. Some of the issues raised in movement publications, such as how to enable women with children to take part in the movement, or the question of childcare in the workplace, reflect a vivid awareness of the demands of everyday life.

A housewife member of Group "Fighting Women" spoke her mind in a tone rather different from that of the "housewife debate" mentioned in chapter 2:

> You men think you're lord and master at home, but who do you owe that to? You just sire the kids, and then what do you care, looking after 'em is a woman's job. You shut her up at home, and think you're keeping her? Three free meals and an afternoon nap thrown in? You gotta be kidding! Just minding the house without doing anything fetches a good price these days. And if we get pregnant, and we're stuck with having the kid and so we bring it up with loving care, that makes us overprotective "education mamas." You leave us nothing to live for and then you add insult to injury!
> Protect the *ie*, defend the nation, produce more young people for the sake of Japan's future, ban abortion to protect public morals. Have more children?—count me out. Whoever heard of such a stupid line of work?. . .[16]

It did not follow, however, that women's lib began calling for a proper evaluation of housewives' labor. Instead, they denounced tax reforms which gave preferential status to married women.[17] For although the starting point of women's lib was self-affirmation, if women were to affirm themselves completely, they had to fundamentally question and reject illusions about women's roles, including those of housewife, wife, and mother. In the process, it was often argued that the images of women are polarized into the wife and mother versus the whore as the opposite ends of a continuous spectrum.

> The patient submission of wives and mothers supports the entire system. The time has come to reject the virtue of meekness.[18]

> By pressing men and authority in the struggle, I want to dismantle my own internalized illusions about love, husbands and wives, men, purity, children, the home, maternal love, and the like. What I want is to work toward the formation of an autonomous subject, while at the same time helping men in their formation of an autonomous subject.[19]

To men, women fall into one of two categories of image: either the tender mother, or a lust disposal unit = the toilet. . . . Male consciousness owes its polarization to that structure of consciousness which denies sexuality and sees it as dirty.[20]

Thus, when Group "Fighting Women," among others, organized a rally "in solidarity with women who kill their children," it was in recognition that the holy mother at the positive pole of women's roles is also a potential child-killer. She has been forced to accept "a self that is not herself" and lacerated by "the emptiness of 'not living.'"[21]

The idealization of the mother is at the heart of the various fantasy images of women, and it is probably the most powerful of the stereotypes which are internalized by and constrain women themselves. Women's lib repeatedly criticized the idealized image of the mother. Sometimes this criticism was in protest of the pain endured by the woman who had to give up being her true self in order to be a good mother. At other times it took the viewpoint of the child, attacking the imposition of a mother love which tried to mold the child to the mother's wishes.

How to live with a child. . . . this is the eternal question faced by all women who have children. But make no mistake: it is not a matter of living *with a child*, it is a matter of *living* with a child. In no way is the child a woman's only raison d'être, nor is the mother the child's. A way of living is needed in which both the child and the woman can feel truly alive.[22]

The 19 years I spent at home as "our little—," being carefully trained to fit your image of the ideal woman, are starting to come crashing down. . . .
I was afraid of you.
I could never think of going against your wishes. And so I never got to eat cheap candy, I took a dislike to everything you disliked, and I didn't even invite my friends home because I knew you would disapprove.[23]

THE DISSOLUTION OF THE FAMILY

The movement's attention turned, further, to contesting the institution of marriage which forces women to live partial lives, and the institution of the family as a supporting pillar of the establishment.

> Regarding whether or not to give birth, the institution of marriage is a major source of oppression and forced decisions. . . . From [unmarried] women it withholds recognition of their capacity to bear children, which is part of the potential for motherhood, which is part of being female; at the same time it forces these capacities upon [married] women.[24]

> We women exist for men as sexual objects, and for the state as instruments who, in the context of the *ie*, ensure by bearing children that first we and then men are co-opted into the system, and who also indirectly serve the interests of capitalists by doing the unpaid work known as housework. Thus the struggle for our liberation is likely to unfold in unison with the liberation of Eros—that is, a revolution in the prevailing negative attitudes toward sexuality—and also with the struggle of child-care workers, whose work is the first step in raising children as members of society; and the direction it is likely to take is the dissolution of the *ie*.[25]

Virtually every issue of *Onna Eros* carried a wide array of women's experiences and reflections on these experiences. Special issues such as "Dissecting the Housewife's Situation" (no. 6) and "Toward the Dissolution of the Family" (no. 13) brought together accounts of relationships with men, childbirth, abortion, marriage, discord with husbands and mothers-in-law, fresh starts, setbacks, and hopes. In essence, each article was also a practical record of the dissolution of the *ie*.

Among the wealth of personal accounts, one in particular stands out in my mind. Though not published until 1979, it is worth citing at this point. "A Continuing Attempt to Dismantle the Family" by Sakamoto Yoshie appeared in the general-interest magazine *Shiso no kagaku* (The science of ideas).[26] Sakamoto and her partner shared the housework and child care equitably and were described as an ideal working couple—and yet somehow, she writes, it was heavy going. "I wanted to remake our relationship after first destroying the one we had as a married couple." And so, after legally divorcing, at times they lived apart and each had other romantic relationships, and at times they lived together again. At all times, they cooperated in raising their son. At one point their son boarded at a primary school in England, and her ex-husband took leave from his job and went to Spain. When he returned, he moved into the apartment next to hers. Sakamoto writes that they chose to dismantle their family not because it was an oppressive one, but because the very fact of being a family was in itself oppressive. . . . What made this article so striking were the depth of its author's radical questioning of the family, the tenacity with which she kept on experimenting, as it were, and her complete honesty.

Dissolution of and experimentation with the family became something of a trend in the seventies. Communes, or non-familial groups living collectively, formed around the country. Such themes were taken up by the mainstream media also, and appeared frequently in magazines and movies. In addition to independent movies such as *Kyokushiteki eros: Koiuta* 1974 (Private Eros: Love song 1974), which included a scene where the heroine's ex-husband films the birth of the child she is having with her lover, there were also commercially successful films like *Seishun no satsujinsha* (Murderer of youth) (1976), which depicts a young man's murder of his parents. The 1980s saw a second boom of movies on the theme of dissolution of the family, but this time they were more detached and comical. Those made in the seventies were, it seems to me, both more direct and more disturbing.

THE TWO WAVES OF FEMINISM

So far, I have tried to represent the positions of women's lib in the words of its supporters, based on primary sources. Finally, let us take a longer view and examine the relationship between changes in the family and the women's lib movement.[27]

Historically, the feminist movement has consisted of two great waves. The first arose toward the end of the nineteenth century and continued, in the West, until around the end of the First World War. There followed, in the West, a hiatus of fifty years before what is known as the "second wave." (Why this hiatus lasted so long is something of a mystery; in the next section, we will look at one possible explanation.)

The history of the Japanese women's movement is usually divided into "prewar" and "postwar" eras. Certainly, Japan's defeat in World War II and the ensuing Occupation marked a turning point, since women's suffrage and other significant advances were achieved at this time. However, these same changes had in fact been sought by the Japanese women's movement since the Taisho Period (1912–1926). When one considers the nature of the changes sought during the two phases of the movement in Japan, it seems more appropriate to use the terms "first wave" for the earlier phase (pre-World War II to the immediate postwar years), and "second wave" for the phase which began in the 1970s with women's lib. In this and the following section, we will look at how the two waves differed in content.

As we saw earlier, in modern society the public and private spheres are separated. The first wave of the feminist movement, whether in Japan or the West, focused its attention chiefly on the public domain, i.e., politics and economics. One major goal was the right to vote—the quintessential political issue. In the economic sphere, the feminists of the first wave did not press for all women to work outside the home. They were mainly concerned with securing decent conditions for those working-class women who had no choice but to work.

On the whole, first-wave feminists did not define as core issues women's roles as housewives, wives, and mothers. There were some influential members in the early years who opposed the institution of marriage and advocated sexual freedom. These elements lost strength, however, after meeting not only with a storm of public outrage but also with ostracism from fellow feminists who regarded them as holding the movement back.

Far from contesting women's domestic role, those in the mainstream came to base their case for improvement of women's status on the supposedly feminine qualities which were closely associated with this role. Having made little headway campaigning for equality with men, the suffrage movement gradually shifted its ground. Once woman had the franchise, they argued, her superior moral character, her innately emotional and caring nature could remedy what was lacking in cold modern-day society. If women participated in decision-making, they held, world peace and the greater good of society were assured.[28]

Jo Freeman, a sociologist who has studied the feminist movement, sums up its early course in this way: "Although originally a broad and diverse movement concerned with all aspects of a woman's life, toward the end it attracted primarily two kinds of feminists—the suffragist and the reformist."[29] Reformists (also called "maternalists") were those who wanted to improve society through women's moral influence. Women's role in the home became the crucial link between reformists and suffragists. With regard to women's domestic role, the mainstream of the first wave eventually arrived at a position which not only recognized but actively affirmed the status quo and utilized it to gain equality in the public sphere. The second wave, however, would question the role itself.

FEMINISM AND THE MODERN FAMILY

The Feminine Mystique by Betty Friedan ignited the women's liberation movement in the United States.[30] In her 1963 best-seller, Friedan describes how, having advanced steadily toward her goal of becoming a psychologist, earning excellent grades up to graduate school, she was suddenly overcome with fear. It occurred to her that if she continued as she was, she might never marry—and that was where a woman's true happiness lay. So she gave up her academic ambitions, married, and became a suburban housewife raising three children. However, she soon found herself in the grip of "the problem that has no name," wondering just who she was. A job as a magazine interviewer brought her into contact with women of her own generation, and in talking to them she discovered that the same distress was gnawing at many contemporary American women. This led her to ask why they were so unhappy when they had an ideal home life. Searching for the answer deep inside herself, she wrote the book which evoked a storm of response from housewives who discovered they were not alone. Friedan went on to become a leader of the National Organization for Women (NOW).

The fifties in America were the age of the housewife. Women had filled a wide range of jobs during World War II, but had been ousted by the returning GIs at the war's end. The second wave of American feminism was, undoubtedly, a direct reaction to the pressure on women to stay at home in the name of "the modern family."

In an earlier book, I offered a hypothesis concerning the relationship between feminism and the modern family.[31] It can be summarized as follows. As we saw in chapter 5, the particular historical entity which we know as "the modern family" became established in the European middle classes during the nineteenth century, and spread to all classes by about the 1920s. Its rise was accompanied by a clear demarcation of public and private spheres, assigned respectively to men and to women. But the emergence of this new social order was initially marked by confusion over the rules. What was the appropriate role for each sex? What kind of mutual relationship should they create? Which was the more important, their equality as human beings, or the differences between the sexes? It was out of this confusion, I suggest, that the first wave of feminism arose.

Gradually, however, as the system in which men occupied the public sphere and women the private sphere stabilized, only that form of feminism which did not conflict with this system survived. The equality it sought was merely formal. In reality, the movement accepted that the sexes occupied segregated niches. The confusion subsided, and the modern family system remained unchallenged for the next five decades.

When confusion over the rules once again developed, the second wave of feminism arose. This time, however, society was changing in a different direction: now it was not the formation but the breakdown of the modern family system that was at hand. Hence the women's liberation movement questioned both the domestic role of women and the dichotomy between public and private spheres. One could say that women's lib presaged the end of an era.

In Japan, however, due to the circumstances we have seen in earlier chapters, the situation was more complicated. Movement writers frequently used the phrase "dissolution of the *ie*" in ways which suggest that they had conflated the *ie* and the modern family until they were unsure which one they wanted to dismantle.

Clearly, the main targets of their specific criticisms were women's roles in the modern family (as housewives, wives, and mothers), and to this extent their position was unmistakably on a new and different level from the early postwar democratizers' call for "liberation from the *ie*." At the same time, however, Japanese women's lib resembled its early postwar forebears in devoting a considerable part of its energies (especially in the detailed personal confessions mentioned earlier) to cursing the *ie* system and its sticky web of relationships—for example, the relations between wife and mother-in-law, or the emphasis on lineage.

The picture becomes still more complex when we note that, in advocating sex as communication, arguably women's lib was seeking the full realization of one of the ideals of the modern family, namely, the union of the sexes through true love and sex.[32] Liberation from the *ie*, and liberation from the family: this dual problem would be carried over into the next era.

| "New Family" Meets the Housewife's Malaise

WHAT BECAME OF THE BABY BOOMERS?

In the previous chapter, we discussed the women's liberation movement. In this chapter, we will shift to a slightly later time frame but still focus on more or less the same generation: women who were in their early twenties during the peak years of women's lib, 1970–72, regardless of whether they were active in the movement or not. This age group is centered on the *dankai no sedai*, the "clumped generation" of Japan's postwar baby boom who were born between 1947 and 1949. What were these women's lives like from the mid-70s onward?

Soon after women's lib peaked, the term *nyu famiri* (new family) entered the language. Today the phrase is largely of historical interest, although one still hears it used on occasion to mean "a family of a new type," but in its day, "new family" was a very popular buzzword. The image it conjured up was promoted by TV commercials such as Marui Department Store's "*waki aiai*" (happy harmony) and "*aijo hatsuratsu*" (full of love and life) campaigns, and the food manufacturer Kikkoman's "*fufu de wain*" (drinking wine together as a married couple).

In a survey I made of contemporary newspapers and magazines, I found that the term occurred most frequently in 1976 and 1977. For example, the article "A Complete Report on the New Family," in the June 13, 1977 issue of *Heibon Panchi*, opens like this:

You could call it an American look: a young couple dressed in similar stylish clothes, just right for a stroll. Then you notice they've got a child with them, dressed the same way: the whole family is wearing perfectly coordinated outfits. Lately such families are everywhere.

Reflecting this booming interest, the 1976 *White Paper on the National Life* took a comparative look at the new family and what it called the *orudo famiri* (old family). The study defined "new family" as follows: "The term evidently refers to young married couples in general, and particularly young married couples born after the war who have a new way of thinking and who show this by their behavior."[1] The children who did not know war (in the words of a sixties pop song), the members of the generation which had been active in women's liberation and the student movement were now several years farther down the road, and they were said to be creating new families full of love and life.

Although derived from English, the Japanese term seems to have taken on a complex significance of its own. What, then, was the *nyu famiri*?

THE MYTH OF THE NEW FAMILY

Before examining the "new family" phenomenon with the benefit of hindsight, let us first see how it was understood at the time. Over a period of several months in 1976, the major daily newspaper *Asahi Shimbun* carried a series titled "When Postwar Babies Marry." Eight of the articles were devoted to the new family.[2] The first article cited the following behavioral traits as being typical of the new family, in implicit contrast with the traditional family: "They do things together as a couple and include the children whenever possible, they share the housework, and they act just like friends. They are fashion-conscious and love to wear jeans. They keep up with pop music and enjoy leisure activities and dining out. At first glance, they appear to be hedonists who live for the moment." The husband in the families discussed was almost always a white-collar corporate employee, and dual-income couples were reported to be common.

As in all the articles about new family couples written at this time, the first point the series made was that their consumption patterns differed from those of previous generations: for example, they bought wine. Today there is nothing startling about this, but once only those who socialized with Westerners would have done such a thing. Thus, reports that people in their twenties were casually drinking wine at home with their meals created quite a sensation. The change could be partly attributed to the Westernization of daily life, as seen in the shift to a dining table and chairs instead of the low table traditionally used on a tatami floor, but this did not seem to entirely explain the new behavior. Many theories were put forward. For example, this generation was said to be less preoccupied with the actual food on their tables and more interested in creating atmosphere, because they had grown up amidst plenty. Alternatively, in an implied contrast with the traditional husband drinking saké at home in the evenings, served but not joined by his wife, it was suggested that young couples were drinking wine together because, for them, meals had become a time for shared relaxation and communication.

These new consumers, it was reported, would spare no expense to acquire things they liked for their tastefully coordinated homes, but rejected anything that didn't appeal to their tastes, even if it was free. They bought what they wanted when they wanted it, even if it meant going into debt by using credit or a loan, which was not common practice at that time. And they favored a casual style which also departed from established conventions. These changes in consumer habits, associated with a new lifestyle, were considered the primary identifying trait of the new family.[3]

Another point often noted together with these consumption patterns was the trend toward equality in the marriage relationship, or what was known as the *tomodachi fufu* (friend-couple, or married couple who are friends—a pairing of two concepts not previously associated in Japanese).[4]

Although they were no doubt partly staged, the photos of new family couples which illustrated the newspaper series were so typical of this trend that they are almost funny. If one partner wore jeans, both wore jeans; if one wore a casual sweater, both did. Their clothing was often unisex and very similar in style, although not actual matching outfits. And they certainly sounded like the best of friends as they told the interviewer, "We were college classmates. In fact, we're the same age."

These featured couples typified their generation in several ways. Before the war there had been a difference of 4 years between the average male and female ages at first marriage; by the 1970s, this was down to 2.7 years.[5] Thirty-six percent of respondents in a 1976 survey of younger couples had met their spouse at the place where they both worked, 12 percent had met through other job-related contacts, and 17 percent had met at school or college.[6] Clearly, there had been a real increase in marriages between classmates or colleagues of the same or similar age. Further, when asked what they viewed as important in a marriage partner, the husbands in the survey ranked "a similar sense of values" first, while the wives ranked this second.[7] Commentators pointed to an increase in the number of couples who acted like friends even after marriage and saw their spouse as someone with whom they could talk freely. Among other reported traits of the new family, partners were said to be calling each other by their personal names or pet names, (whereas their parents addressed each other either by different second-person pronouns associated with unequal status, or else by "Mother" and "Father").[8] The husbands were also said to be doing more than the customary amount of housework. A related survey found that, compared to older age groups, married men in their twenties did more shopping, cooking, clearing up after meals, cleaning, and laundry.[9]

This is what we might have expected of the women's lib generation, and such findings seem to suggest that the effects of the movement were showing up already. But the story was, in reality, considerably more complicated.

The fate of the new family is a legend—or a lesson—which is still handed down in the marketing industry. First, there was the sensation created by its debut. The retail industry, which was then in the grip of a recession, jumped at the potential profits represented by the large population of baby boomers, and department stores began to offer an array of products developed to suit their supposedly different consumer preferences. Displays were designed to emphasize a unified sense of style. Two magazines were launched for the new family: *Kurowassan* (Croissant) and *Aruru*. But the truth of the matter is that these new products and publications did not sell.

After about a year, the promotional enthusiasm suddenly gave way to accusations that the new family had never existed—that it was "a phantom."[10] According to a survey by the Japan News Network Data Bank, it was actually middle-aged couples who were buying the wine and the Western-style pastries. A survey by Daihyaku Mutual Life Insurance found also that the younger generation were taking out life insurance and keeping up savings on the installment plan at rates comparable to their elders.[11] Even Marui Department Store, an early herald of the supposed trend, shifted in June 1977 from the "new family" approach which it had been pursuing for five years to a *nyu yangu* (new young) line. The store's president put the problem this way: "The 'new families' were good customers until they had children. Now they are having to spend so much on their children that they can no longer afford to buy things."

Since it was so quickly declared a phantom, there have been remarkably few scientific surveys or studies on the subject of the "new family."[12] Let us see if we can discover the true nature of the phenomenon that went by this name.

"FRIEND-COUPLES"?

The prime example of an unsuccessful product which targeted the new family is the magazine *Croissant*. It faltered after a gala launching under such slogans as "the lifestyle magazine for the new family—the magazine couples read together," and there were rumors that it was about to close down after a year. But the publishers were not to be defeated. In *Croissant*'s second year they revamped it, boosted its circulation, and turned it into a trendsetter. This remodeling may supply some clues as to the true nature of what was being called the "new family."

First, let us look at *Croissant* when it was not selling. The cover of the May 1977 inaugural issue was emblazoned with the magazine's slogans against a colorful background of artwork. Inside, its central concerns were not very different from those of traditional women's magazines (housework, child rearing, fashion, etc.), but some articles in the early issues reveal a distinctive angle—for example, "Housework Is a Job for a Man" (October 1977). One typical feature was interviews with couples who personified the new family—even advertisements often took the form of simulated interviews. The July 1977 issue contains a good example, in this case an actual interview. It was accompanied by photographs of Mikki, the longhaired husband, and Ichiko, the wife, who wore almost no makeup, shown hugging each other or snug in bed. The text presents their relationship in terms of a passionate love affair, from how they met, through the three years they lived together before getting married, to the present day ("We're still crazy about each other"). These two were surely a perfect example of the "friend-couple," or even of what is called (with a similar sense, in Japanese, of a contradiction in terms) *koibito-fufu*, a married couple who are lovers.

To our eyes today, however, there is something odd about the friend-couples who appear in the early issues of *Croissant*. For example, take figure 7-1. This photograph was part of a promotion for Iona cosmetics in the same July 1977 issue. It shows a couple riding double on a bicycle, dressed casually in jeans and T-shirts. They are the very picture of a "friend-couple," but look at how they are posed. He is the one pedaling, while she leans against him and dangles her feet. If he were to suddenly remove himself, she would fall flat on the ground. At first glance the couple appears to be equal, the wife as freewheeling as the husband. But in fact it is he who pedals the matrimonial bicycle, and she is entirely supported by him.

This is just one of many allusions to male dominance in the visual representation of the new family. It may seem that we are

Fig. 7-1.
Source: Croissant, July 1977.

reading too much into a photograph—after all, it could have just turned out that way, or been posed that way merely by chance. But the decision to publish a particular image reflects both the editors' intentions and the tacit assumptions they share with readers, and it is worthwhile to analyze the images from this point of view.[13]

Figure 7-1 is unintentionally revealing of a certain limit set by *Croissant*'s editors. That is to say, they must have judged, whether consciously or unconsciously, that this was about as far as they could go in depicting equality and "friend-couples" without readers being offended.

What are the "new family" wives described as doing? All we learn about Ichiko is that she is making a special effort with her cooking. The wife in figure 7-1, according to the ad copy, "says that when she got married she didn't hesitate to give up her job as a graphic designer in order to stay at home." She dreams of maybe taking up the electronic organ again, and going on family vacations. Several of the husbands are identified as rock or jazz musicians, and—perhaps reflecting the trendiness of this type—many are said to have quit the corporate world to become self-employed. By featuring these men, such articles were clearly promoting a way of life that valued the home and private life—and yet they contained almost no ideas for a new way of life for women.

As mentioned earlier, there have been few factual studies of the new family. One of the few available resources is a "Survey of Recent Attitudes among Married Couples" which was conducted for the women's page of the *Asahi Shimbun* in 1976.[14] The subjects were married residents of a housing complex in the Tokyo Metropolitan Area, and the findings provide valuable clues to the actual relationship of the new family's "friend-couples." As we have already seen in an early reference to this survey, marriages between co-workers and classmates were common. It was also noted earlier that the husbands ranked "a similar sense of values" as the most important condition for marriage; this was followed by "compatible interests" and "the approval of my/our parents." The wives' priorities were, in descending order: "future prospects," "a similar sense of values," and "my/our parents' approval." Even in these "friend-couples," the wives evidently did not question the alignment of their own future happiness with their husbands' prospects. Also, the ideals expressed by both sexes, when asked what kind of partner they wanted to have and what kind of partner they wanted to be, were a "sweet" wife and a "dependable" husband, but the women seem to have been more strongly in favor of both of these stereotypes than the men.

Respondents were also asked whether they agreed with the International Women's Year Action Group's protest against the "I'm the one who cooks/I'm the one who eats" commercial, which was then currently in the news. The IWY Action Group had protested a TV commercial for instant ramen which featured the lines: "I'm the one who cooks" and "I'm the one who eats" (with feminine and masculine pronouns, respectively), bringing a critical perspective on the sexual division of labor to general public awareness. Fifty percent of the wives and 30 percent of the husbands in the survey expressed understanding, while 40 percent of the wives and 60 percent of the husbands disagreed with the protesters. Thus, there was a noticeable difference in men's and women's views on the gender-determined division of labor. Yet, while they may have had some vague doubts about gender roles, the women covered by this survey clearly had not shed the desire to be sweet wives who depended on their husbands.

THE SHORT LIFE OF THE MODERN FAMILY

At this point, I would like to refer back to the graph of the labor force participation rate of women, by age and generation (figure 1-2). Group C, the cohort born in 1946–50, are the women who were said to have created the new family. This was the generation in which the M-shaped curve had the deepest dip; that is, it was the generation in which the greatest proportion of married women became full-time housewives. Thus, in a sense it was only natural for *Croissant*'s writers to equate married women with full-time housewives. Although the *Asahi Shimbun* had pointed to the number of dual-income couples as a characteristic of the new family, in reality this was true only of the brief period before the birth of their first child. We should also note that the change in consumption patterns observed after these couples had children was no doubt due in part to the loss of the wife's income.

There is thus a certain irony in the fact that this group has been dubbed the "new family" generation, for while they envisioned marriage as an equal partnership, in reality they had a smaller economic base for equality than previous generations. Their apparent self-contradiction may seem less puzzling, however, if we realize that the whole concept of the new family was premised on a gendered division of labor: the husband worked and the wife stayed at home, but they were to remain equals nevertheless. As we saw in *Croissant*, the image of the new family that was being constructed in the media presented almost no challenge to existing gender roles.

It might be better, then, to view the concept of the new family as a step toward "liberation from the *ie*" rather than, in the terms of chapter 6, "liberation from the family." Perhaps it can best be understood as an attempt to build a democratic family held together by bonds of love, with equality between the partners and between parents and children; in short, the modern family as an aspiration of postwar democracy. Although the first generation to marry after the war had been unable to realize this ideal completely, it was hoped that the next generation would be the one to do so. This view is borne out by the fact that, according to the *Asahi Shimbun* series, the obstacles encountered by the new family were typically *ie*-related. These included the question of family names, and the bride's clashes with her mother-in-law and the values of the generation she represented.

Going back a little further in time, we can gain a sense of what "new family" couples were like before they married. The cultural trend known as sexual liberation, which dated from the student rebellion in 1968, popularized a sexy image of the female body daringly exposed in such fashions as mini-skirts and see-through blouses. Although this image also comes to us via the media, unlike the new family it seems to have been more than a media creation. But look at the photograph in figure 7-2, which appeared in an ad in the April 29–May 6, 1968 issue of the mass-circulation weekly *Josei jishin* (Woman herself). It is a shot of a young woman who has just been approached by an attractive man. She wears a short dress with a bold floral print. But note her extremely self-conscious posture, with toes turned in and fists clenched. The scene has been choreographed to make the point that, at heart, she is such a shy girl that she freezes at a moment like this. Advertising photography in magazines from 1968 to about 1970 often made

Fig. 7-2.
Source: Josei jishin, April 29–May 6, 1968.

use of the same kind of effect: an imbalance between provocative dress and extremely demure gestures.[15] The message seems to be that women had become sexy, but only to get themselves chosen by men. Given this background, one can understand all the more clearly the impatience of the women's movement toward sexual liberation of the *Heibon Panchi* type. For far from freeing women, sexual liberation as practiced by the tabloid magazines merely exposed them more blatantly than ever as sexual objects before the male gaze.

Urged on by the rallying cry of sexual liberation, young men and women had romantic relationships which sometimes included sexual relations, and even lived together. The rate of premarital intercourse first begins to rise, slowly but steadily, in the generation that was young in the early seventies.[16] Nevertheless, the expectation that the man would take the initiative remained unchanged. Moreover, many of these couples soon took their place within the institution of marriage, and the women became full-time housewives as if it were a matter of course.

What the baby boomers were attempting, then, turns out to have been a realization of the ideal of the modern family in the purest form ever seen in Japan: that is, a marriage in which the bonds were formed by love and sex, and the creation of a family comprised of equal personal relationships together with a division of labor. It was also at this time that love marriages began to outnumber arranged marriages (figure 7-3). As the women's lib movement had realized, however, perfecting the modern family would not bring about Utopia.

Earlier, I spoke of reports that the new family had been a phantom. But while business and media people—who were interested in the new family as consumers—declared outright that it had never existed, sociologists reached a somewhat different assessment, even at the time.

Yuzawa Yasuhiko put it like this: "In the 1920s, the sociologist Ernest Watson Burgess stated that in American society the family was in transition 'from institution to companionship,' and it seems that half a century later the true 'companionate family' has finally emerged in Japan, too . . . . Clearly, never before has so

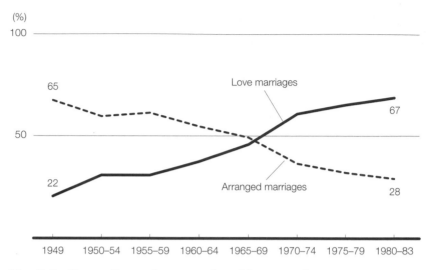

Fig. 7-3. Proportions of arranged and love marriages

Source: Ministry of Health and Welfare, *Kekkon ni Kansuru Jinkogakuteki Chosa*, (Demograph Research on Marriage), 1983

large a mass of young people supported the move to overturn traditional marriage and live a couple-centered lifestyle of their own choosing, without worrying about society's opinion. This is a landmark in the history of the Japanese family."[17]

Izeki Toshiaki compared the new family with *mai homu shugi* or "my-home-ism," the principle of a home- and family-centered life, which had been much talked about in the sixties: "My-home-ism smacked slightly of a guilty conscience in its implied contrast to the *moretsu shain* (dedicated company man). Further, as indicated by the word 'home,' it suggested material fulfillment in terms of a house and consumer durables. In the case of the new family, however, there is no sense of guilt. The new family is conceived of in terms of its members rather than the home. In all areas of daily life, such as shopping and leisure, there is a consciousness of the unit of behavior being the couple and their children."[18]

In a theoretical discussion of Japanese youth, Nakano Osamu arrived at a unique analysis with links to Christopher Lasch's culture of narcissism. Nakano established that because young people (unlike their elders) had grown up in houses having separate bedrooms for the parents and the children, their psychology was so strongly conditioned by having a room of their own that "the private room is part of the self." He goes on to say that "when the occupants of a private space are a married couple, with or without a child, this living space is precisely equivalent to the 'new family.'"[19]

All three of these authors interpreted the new family as that form of the Japanese family which was most radically oriented toward the modern family ideal. As I have already indicated, I am basically in agreement with this view. I cannot bring myself to dismiss everything we know about the new family as a mere phantom.

However, when the golden age of the "companionate family" finally arrived, it did not last for long. Like a fleeting mirage, it vanished as suddenly as it had appeared—not because it was imperfectly realized, as is often claimed, but because once it was realized all of its internal contradictions erupted at once.

Critics of the new lifestyle often disparagingly called it "feminine." Ironically, though, it was women who rose in revolt against the new family.

INDEPENDENCE AND THE HOUSEWIFE'S MALAISE

Now let us look at *Croissant* in its second year. What was the revamped and successful magazine like? The key lies in its new catchphrase: "the woman's newspaper." From a magazine about the new lifestyle intended to be read together by women and men, by wives and husbands, *Croissant* became a lifestyle magazine for women only. In other words, the editorial department gave up on men. They decided that the men of this generation were definitely not new. Only the women were new.

We have already noted a difference in men's and women's attitudes to gender-determined roles. The new family thereafter widened this gap even further. While men seemed to decide the existing power relations were not all that bad and ceased even paying lip service to the ideal, women, it seems, wanted to go on believing in the ideal of friend-couples. In response to its readers' growing interest in a more independent role, the visual images of the new *Croissant* frequently showed working women. Many were not career women, but resourceful former housewives who had started their own business or opened their own store. The stories of these ordinary women were illustrated with big glossy photographs.

Also new were photo features showing women deep in thought, women reading books—images which would once have been considered unattractive, but were now presented in a glamorous way. This was the essence of the new *Croissant*. With "independence" as its watchword, the magazine had an enormous influence on women in the late 70s and early 80s. (Its influence was so great that the term "the *Croissant* syndrome" was later coined as an ironic description of the fate of those who had waited too long to get married while pursuing their independence and thus missed the boat.)

But however much they longed for the life that *Croissant* depicted, once the women of the new family had quit their jobs to stay home, independence was not within their immediate reach. The anguish this caused was well described in the 1982 best-seller *Tsumatachi no shishuki* (The autumnal crisis of married women) by Saito Shigeo.[20] *Shishuki* is a word invented by the author on the analogy of *shishunki*, adolescence, which literally means "thinking-of-spring period" (with "spring" having erotic connotations in Japanese). Saito replaced "spring" (*shun*) with "autumn" (*shu*), and suggested in his book that women experienced more angst in the autumn of life than in its spring. He was referring to the experience of women who, after marrying and devoting themselves to homemaking, reached a point where their children no longer needed much attention and suddenly said to themselves: "I'm not young any more. What am I doing? Haven't I got anything better to do?" This malaise, which struck when the children reached elementary or junior high school age, was the *shishuki*. Clearly, the symptoms are very like those identified by Betty Friedan among American women in the 1950s.

As the book's case studies show, at the beginning of the 1980s alcoholism among Japanese housewives was recognized as a social problem, also known by such terms as "the kitchen syndrome" and "kitchen drinking." Overcome by vague anxiety, many house-wives did not know what to do with themselves, and could not concentrate on the housework they had formerly managed with ease. At such times they found themselves reaching for the cooking saké there on the kitchen shelf. If a housewife became an alcoholic, her husband might lecture her or tell her to see a doctor, but it would be obvious that he did not understand what was troubling her. "Don't I bring in a regular paycheck?" he might ask. "What more do you want? Why can't you get the housework done?" In the end, many husbands in this situation turned away from their wives and pretended not to notice the dirt accumulating, or eventually stopped coming home at all.

But surely Japanese women's lib had spoken of these problems a decade earlier? In America, the background to the rise of the movement was the discontent of married women in the 1950s, who had all become housewives en masse. In Japan, the same discontent was now striking the women of the baby boom generation, among whom the shift to housewife status had gone further than ever before—in spite of the fact that women's lib had earlier warned of the problems involved.

In 1983, the year after publication of *The Autumnal Crisis of Married Women*, the television drama *Kinyobi no tsumatachi* (Friday's wives), known as *Kintsuma* for short, became a popular topic of conversation. The show's central characters were all baby boomers. The first series revolved around three couples who had experience in the student movement, and the soundtrack featured plenty of Bob Dylan to help establish their background.

Kintsuma is remembered as the classic show in a TV genre known as "adultery dramas," which flourished in the 1980s. It differed in tone from conventional daytime soap operas, which depicted women's extramarital affairs in a more titillating way. The scripts of the early *Kintsuma* episodes had real substance, and perhaps the enthusiastic response to the program can be accounted for by its authentic portrayal of such things as housewives' anxiety, misunderstandings between spouses, and women's friendships.

The circumstances leading to the extramarital affairs were always clearly portrayed. The first series begins with the divorce of a former flight attendant and perfect housewife. She is energetic, methodical, a dedicated "education mama"—but constantly on edge. When her husband can't stand the tension any more, he falls in love with a younger woman. Thus, from the start, the drama dealt with the frustration and restlessness of women at home. The second series presented the situation in a purer form: an ordinary housewife, with no particular complaints about her family or her husband, is drawn toward an affair when she finds that something indefinable is missing.

Both *The Autumnal Crisis of Married Women* and *Friday's Wives* focused attention on the fact that, although the housewife's life had always been regarded by the rest of society as a very comfortable one, being a housewife was in itself a source of dissatisfaction. Public opinion was shocked. When women achieved a wife's status, surely they had a cushy position, with three meals a day and a nap included. And they still weren't happy?

But that was indeed what women's lib had been saying ten years earlier. Though the women of the baby boom might have been expected to have some knowledge of the movement's ideas, they had pursued the elusive vision of the new family and become full-time housewives. A decade or so later, when child care no longer occupied their time, they discovered that they had turned the words of the seventies women's movement into an unhappy reality. This was the trend of the 1980s.

ESCAPE FROM THE HOUSEWIFE'S ROLE

Let us turn once more to the graph of working women by age and generation (figure 1-2) and look at Group C, the baby boomers who stayed home in greater numbers than any other generation of women in Japanese history. What sort of lives have these women led since their cohort passed the lowest point of the M? As an M-shaped curve, of course it rises again after the initial fall—but notice how steeply it rises. It is hardly surprising that the intense energy of this rush to the outside world was accompanied by equally intense confusion and pain.

As the graph shows, the women of Group B, who are ten years older than Group C, had also been gradually returning to employment. But in the baby boom generation the age at which this occurred was skewed forward, and furthermore all the women returned to work at once. The older group had not considered themselves free from looking after their children until around the time the children finished high school; only then did they think about doing something else. But the next generation seems to have considered themselves free at about the time the children entered junior high school. These mothers, in their thirties, still had a genuine chance of finding employment, albeit part-time in many cases. Economic factors also played a part in their desire to take jobs, as male workers' pay increases had leveled off after the oil crisis of 1973, and their wives now had to help with the costs of education and housing.

The return to work was not the only form that this outward movement took. Many women found meaning in other kinds of social involvement, even though these brought in no money. For example, the women of Group B caused a boom in the courses offered by commercially operated "culture centers" on a wide variety of subjects such as languages and art. Also, (more in Group C than Group B), many women became active in the community, and these activities went beyond the realm of hobbies and self-improvement as they became involved in buyers' cooperatives, consumer campaigns, and citizens' movements. Such social activism seems to be characteristic of the younger generations of housewives, starting with the baby boomers. More recently, a number of women have run for office at the national and local levels with the support of this kind of network.

At first, then, it had appeared that the women of the most populous generation had all decided to stay home at the same time, but shortly afterwards they all reemerged at the same time. This rushing back and forth by the vast majority of a generation not only caused them inner turmoil; it also, inevitably, had a major impact on society as a whole.

The eighties were often said to be "the age of women." "Women's independence" was a media buzzword, and there was a widespread impression that women were changing. "Change" for women meant, in a word, getting out of the house, and during the eighties the leading housewives' magazines ceased publication one after another, while such phrases as *okusama-rashiku* (in a manner befitting the lady of the house) and *misesu-rashiku* (in a manner befitting a married woman) disappeared from those that survived.[21] Both in magazines and in real life, it became standard for single and married women to dress indistinguishably. Thus, today a married woman's wardrobe includes shorts, jeans, and denim jackets—a clear expression of a new self-image.

When viewed in the light of these trends among the baby boomers, the public interest that *feminizumu* (feminism) attracted in the eighties can be readily understood as part of the same phenomenon. The field of women's studies, which had been growing since the 1970s, bore fruit at last as feminist scholars produced a steady stream of publications. Moreover, debates on a number of issues drew the attention of a much wider public. These included the controversy over the provisions of the Equal Employment Opportunity Law, enacted in 1985, and the 1987 "Agnes debate," which was sparked when TV personality Agnes Chan began taking her baby to the studio while she worked, and which focused on the rights and wrongs of this individual solution together with the lack of institutional support for working mothers.

Ten years after they had created "new families" in large numbers, the baby-boomer women were finding in their own lives that the predictions of women's lib had been on target. And for a second time women's pain and resentment sought expression in feminist terms. Thus the housewife and domesticity were at the heart of eighties feminist theory in Japan.[22]

THE FUTURE OF THE *HANAKO* GENERATION

So far, we have looked mainly at the baby-boom generation, and have seen that it was the mass escape of housewives in this age group which constituted the *shufubanare* (escape from the housewife role) phenomenon of the 1980s. In this connection, however, we must also note a new trend that has been set in motion by women of a still younger generation. There has recently been a definite increase in the number of women who continue to work into their late twenties or early thirties without marrying. (Such women are sometimes jokingly referred to as "the *Hanako* tribe," after the name of a magazine.)

As we saw in figure 3-3, after remaining stable over an extended period, the average age at first marriage reached a turning point in the mid-1970s and has since risen steeply. Today, women's marriage prospects can no longer be likened to Christmas cakes being sold at a discount after the 24th. Instead, to stretch the metaphor, we could say these women are more like New Year's rice cakes, still in demand at 30 and 31. This younger generation has thus contributed to the phenomenon of escaping from the housewife role by being in no hurry to become housewives in the first place.

Turning again to figure 1-2, note the trajectory of Groups D and E, the cohorts ten and twenty years younger than the baby boomers. As discussed in chapter 1, there has been an actual reversal of the stay-at-home trend in the past decade; that is, in Group D the bottom of the M has rebounded to a higher point than in the older groups, and Group E is on course for an even higher point. Close study of the statistics shows, however, that this is not due to a major increase in women remaining continuously in the workforce throughout their lives. Instead, later marriage has combined with earlier reemployment to shorten the stay-at-home period of full-time housework. In addition, as noted in chapter 3, the average age at first marriage has a greater variance, that is, the normative "appropriate" age of marriage has been relaxed, and the stay-at-home years accordingly vary quite widely among individuals, falling in the early twenties for some people, and the mid-thirties for others. These two trends have combined to fill in the bottom of the M for Groups D and E, that is, women born in the late 1950s and 1960s.[23]

In sum, women younger than the baby boomers have been slow to become housewives. When they do become housewives, it is not for a large portion of their lives. And furthermore, they do not all become housewives at the same time.

A 1987 survey by the Pola Research Institute of Beauty and Culture, operated by the cosmetics sales company Pola, included some interesting findings on generational differences in women's attitudes to the marriage relationship.[24] Unlike the other generations, an overwhelming proportion of baby boomers chose the following multiple-choice option: "A wife should not always defer to her husband but should put heart and soul into her own interests or job and value her own way of life." This was in obvious contrast to the oldest generation, who chose "A wife should be attentive in support of her husband and ensure that he can maintain his dignity as head of the household." But the youngest generation, ten years younger than the baby boomers, showed a different reaction again. They heavily favored: "A wife and husband should share the housework and child care and be mutually supportive of each other's work and activities." Here, a confrontational stance between the sexes had been replaced by a cooperative one. The study's analyst comments: "This probably represents true equality in marriage. That a wife should not defer to her husband but should value her own way of life does not have to be stated explicitly; it is already taken for granted as a major premise. She would not have married in the first place if it meant neglecting her own life."

Thus the "Hanako tribe" generation has not only set a new trend by its actions, but has also made a new departure in its attitudes. A further example is the fact that while the rate of premarital intercourse showed the first signs of rising in the baby boom generation, the real upswing began in the generation immediately following the boomers.[25]

The point I want to make here is that if we are to predict the direction of future changes, we must pay the closest attention to the generations after the baby boomers. When these younger women reach the age of the autumnal crisis, i.e., the mid-thirties to early forties, can they too expect to experience a crisis?

There are, I think, two broad conditions which must be in place before this crisis will occur as a social phenomenon. The first is obvious: women must be at home. A woman must be a housewife to experience the housewife's malaise. In the days when most brides married into small-business or farming households, they had no time to worry about having nothing to do, or what they were going to do next. They were provided with all the work they could handle.

The second condition is a relatively small number of children per couple. If it were not for the trend to smaller families, the housewife might never see the day when her children are all independent. Among the often-cited changes in the typical woman's life cycle, the lessening of child-rearing demands for an increasingly long portion of her life is a change of particular importance. It can be dated from the first generation to marry after the war, who had significantly fewer children than their mothers. Those women, who married in the 1950s and are now in their sixties, are the first generation for which a life of any kind has existed after child rearing. Women before them gave birth to so many children that they arrived at the end of their own life expectancy at about the same time as the youngest child finished growing.

The trend toward becoming housewives and the trend toward couples having fewer children are two of the characteristics I have attributed to the Postwar Family System, and it was these exact same conditions which led to the crisis for housewives. Moreover, this crisis was felt most intensely in the baby boom generation, where these two characteristics were most typical.

Accordingly, to predict whether or not such a crisis awaits today's young women we need to consider whether these two conditions will continue to apply in the future. Smaller families are plainly here to stay—I would guess that hardly anyone today is thinking of having five or six children. The key question, then, is whether women will continue to stay at home. Even as they talked of the "new family," the baby boomers nearly all turned into full-time housewives, to their eventual regret. Are today's young women showing signs of doing the same thing?

I have described at some length how the *Hanako* generation has taken a different approach to work from previous generations. Recently, however, a worrying trend has appeared even among the

Hanakos. The labor force participation rate of Group D, who are now in their early 30s, is falling. This is due to the combined effects of economic recession and their arrival at an age at which they are now taking the long-delayed step of marriage. The resulting small increase in the birthrate for 1994 seems to have been greeted with joy in some government circles, but when one thinks of the women concerned, this is cause for alarm. The "new family" generation of women was essentially the first in Japan that was beset, as a group, by "the problem that has no name," and as a result they went through an agonizing struggle to identify the problem for themselves. But later generations have had ample opportunity to learn from them. It would be a shame if they were to repeat the same sufferings in spite of these women's valuable experience, which has taught us both the cause of the housewives' discontent and its solution.

Chapter 8

Are Today's Parents Bad Parents?

THE CRISIS OF THE FAMILY REVISITED

When I ask people to comment on the state of the family today, a subject which frequently comes up is poor parenting. In fact, this is brought up just as often as the subject of women leaving the housewife role, which I discussed in the previous chapter. Typical comments include: "Parents these days can't even bring up their children properly. Really, I don't know what things are coming to," and "Parents these days lack *bosei* (maternal qualities)." Since the word *bosei* normally applies only to mothers, people sometimes employ a newly coined term, *oyasei* (parental qualities). They may use this term, for example, in suggesting that there is a need for educational programs for parenthood.

A recent series of newspaper articles on the subject of poor parenting complained of mothers' increasing reliance on child-care manuals. One article cited the extraordinary case of a mother whose baby drank less than the average number of ounces of formula, and so she forced it to drink the full average amount, with the result that the baby learned to put its fingers down its throat and bring it all up.

According to the journalist's analysis, such extreme behavior reflects the fact that the contemporary generation of parents has grown up under the pervasive influence of the *hensachi*. This statistical value, the deviation, is used throughout the Japanese education system to measure each student's performance relative to the average score on standardized tests, and has a decisive influence on students' educational future.

125

By this logic, however, all contemporary Japanese will be unfit parents, because all will be members of the *hensachi* generation. Such sweeping social commentary is no help in actually bringing up children. And one does not want to be too quick to blame parents. Instead, we need to examine why they find themselves so widely condemned today.

In chapter 3 I discussed the term "maternally induced diseases" and explained that it refers to the increasing incidence of psychosomatic problems in childhood (such as asthma and stammering). I suggested that these problems were the result of the decrease in the number of children per couple, which had led parents to concentrate their love and attention so intensely on each child that this love had proved to be a burden. The condition can thus be seen as a chronic ailment of the modern family. The completion of the modern family system has not only given rise to the affliction of housewives known as the "autumnal crisis"; it has also had deleterious effects on children.

This was, however, my own interpretation of the phenomenon which Kyutoku Shigemori named "maternally induced diseases." His explanation had quite a different emphasis, as indicated by his choice of name. The main point of Kyutoku's argument was that such diseases are caused by a breakdown of mothers' child-rearing instincts which he believed had occurred under the impact of rapid social change in the era of high economic growth. Among the danger signs mothers may recognize in themselves, he said, are not liking children very much, preferring a small family, enjoying work outside the home more than child care, and having no particular qualms about leaving young children (from infancy to age three) in the care of others.[1]

Kyutoku believed that such a breakdown of child-rearing instincts not only led to illnesses in children, but also represented a pathological change—what he called a "disease of civilization"—in mothers themselves. When regarded in this light, the women of *uman ribu*, who had complained that when a woman became a mother she was forced to accept "a self that is not herself," could be declared sick. Clearly, Kyutoku's 1979 book was employing the familiar line of argument which lays all the family's problems at the door of women's independence.

During the 1980s a broad spectrum of problems in the family aroused public concern. The crisis of married women was the first such issue in the news. This was followed by the rising divorce rate; the growing number of elderly people living alone; and problems among children, including bullying, suicides, and violence against family members. Phrases such as the "dissolution" or "breakdown" of the family became media buzzwords. But where the women's movement had used them with a sense of optimism, the same phrases now took on a tone of alarm as the perception spread that the family was in crisis. Following the Ohira Cabinet's 1979 proposals for "strengthening the foundations of the home," in 1983 a special edition of the *White Paper on the National Life* was devoted to the family, while among the annually published New Social Indicators, "family life" was reported to be the only area showing continuous deterioration.[2]

The cause of this imminent crisis was generally put down to the family's having deviated from its true and desirable form. Women's increasing independence was frequently singled out for criticism because it was seen as representative of the undesirable changes that were taking place in the family.

It is this view of the true form of the family which I have set out to question in this book. As we saw in chapter 5, underlying the perception of crisis in the family is the presumption that the modern family embodies a universal ideal. However, once we realize that the modern form of the family is just one of many historical types, it becomes possible to observe objectively the direction in which change is taking us and contemplate how to respond, rather than acting as if humanity itself were on the brink of disaster.

As a way of framing the issues involved in mother-child relationships, "maternally induced diseases" were a classic example of the alarmist approach. Kyutoku saw a breakdown of what he called "mothers' child-rearing instincts"—which by definition ought to be impossible to lose—under the impact of civilization or social change.

In this chapter, I intend to look into the changing understanding of mother-child interactions in some depth, as a case study of the so-called crisis of the family. In doing so, I hope to show that different conceptual frameworks—the conventional one which informed Kyutoku's diagnosis, and the one I am proposing in this book—lead to different theoretical constructs and interpretations of reality.

THE MYTH OF THE FIRST THREE YEARS

In *Maternally Induced Diseases*, Kyutoku recommended that, if at all possible, parents should avoid placing children in day care until the age of three. The experience of being repeatedly abandoned each morning by the mother, he warned, is unbearably painful for the infant and leaves emotional wounds in later life.

This is, of course, a restatement of a widely held and enormously influential position: that a child should be at its mother's side for the first three years of life. One hears this dictum passed on in many settings, not only by professional experts but by mothers to their daughters, mothers-in-law to daughters-in-law, husbands to wives, and self-appointed dispensers of advice to young mothers in their neighborhood.

Not even the young women of the *Hanako* generation have escaped the power of this magical incantation. In areas other than motherhood, the *Hanakos* have started a new trend by taking for granted the value of their own independent way of life. But when they have children, they too want to shower them with all the love they can give, dress them to look as cute as can be, and provide them with the very best education. The myth of motherhood expressed in the rule of the first three years appears to be even more tenacious than the myth which supports the housewife's role.

As mentioned in previous chapters, several years ago the entertainer Agnes Chan stirred up a controversy by taking her child regularly to her studio workplace. The image of Agnes on her way to work with her baby in her arms seems emblematic of the *Hanako* generation's desire to "have it all."[3] But few women have the privileged status that would make such a solution possible. It even seems to be fairly common for women to decide that, paradoxically, they would rather not have children at all if they have to cut corners in taking care of them; they prefer to remain single or in double-income couples with no kids.

What are the grounds for this insistence on a mother's care until the age of three, which has even the *Hanako* generation under its spell? Its roots go back to psychoanalytic theory. The theories of Freud, which assigned decisive significance to the experiences of infancy, have become very famous indeed. Based on Freud's work, Erik Erikson proposed the concept of developmental stages: that is, there are developmental tasks that must be completed at each stage of life. Unless these tasks have been completed adequately, the individual cannot proceed to the next developmental stage. Since the developmental task of the first stage of life is establishment of basic trust, which is built up through the child's relationship with the mother, Erikson contended that problems in this relationship would lead to harm in later life.

In the United States, when scientism and experimentalism were at their height in the years after World War II, research on human development was centered on mother-child interaction theory, which sought to measure the relationship of mother and child scientifically.[4] The most influential school of thought was attachment theory, whose basic concept was derived from studies of animal behavior. In his book *Solomon's Ring* the ethologist Konrad Lorenz tells an amusing story about being taken for the parent of a clutch of newly hatched greylag geese. Greylag goslings recognize the first moving thing they see as their parent, a behavioral trait which is known as imprinting. John Bowlby, the originator of attachment theory, believed that human beings have a mechanism of attachment which is essentially similar, though not as simple. For example, when a premature baby has been placed in intensive care at birth, the mother may later find it difficult to love the child or handle it with confidence.

With the aid of sophisticated measuring technology, studies based on mother-child interaction theory revealed that the newborn baby, and even the fetus before birth, has considerable capacity to perceive external stimuli. Child-care books written around this time often recommended that mothers begin immediately after birth to talk to the baby, to look into its eyes while nursing, and so on, even if the baby did not yet react.

This school of research certainly made an important contribution by spreading the awareness that babies have the capacity to relate to another person from a very early age. But there was nothing in the experimental results which proved that this other person must be the biological mother, nor that there must be just one person involved. There was nothing which proved this in the results because the early experimenters had decided from the outset that relationships with people other than the mother were not worth considering, and thus had not even attempted to measure them. Conventional assumptions about the modern family had crept into the premises on which the scientists constructed their hypotheses, and had biased their findings. In fact, it has become clear in retrospect that the field of psychoanalysis itself is premised on the interpersonal relationships of the modern family.

The initial tight focus on the mother-child relationship has since become less exclusive in the United States, where researchers' interests have broadened to include the roles of fathers, other caretakers, and other children. The wide-ranging experiments now being done suggest that, provided the baby has interactions with a small number of constant individuals, there is no conclusive evidence in favor of an exclusive relationship with one person—and, of course, men can also be important partners in such interactions.

MATERNAL DEPRIVATION AND EXCESSIVE CLOSENESS OF MOTHER AND CHILD

The work of T.G.R. Bower, while it proceeded directly from orthodox mother-child interaction theory, led the way to a theoretical breakthrough. Since the development of Bower's argument provides a vivid illustration of a shift in theoretical perspective, we will examine it in some detail, taking as an example his analysis of stranger fear and separation anxiety.[5]

Stranger fear (also called stranger anxiety or shyness) refers to the well-known behaviors of small children at the approach of an unfamiliar person: crying, hiding behind their mother or another familiar adult, and so on. Separation anxiety refers to the child's anxiety at the departure of a parent, generally shown by crying and screaming. Neither is a bad thing in itself, for such behavior indicates that a bond of attachment has formed with particular individuals and that the child can distinguish those individuals from others. These are necessary steps in human development. The shyness or anxiety is only a problem when it becomes excessive.

When a child is excessively fearful of strangers and anxious at being left, the mother is often given the following advice: "The problem is that the bond between you and your child is not strong enough. Stay with him and hold him tight. Once you've bonded strongly enough, he will no longer cry and scream when you go out of his sight, because he will be sure you'll always come right back. And he won't be so shy when someone he doesn't know approaches, because he'll feel secure in the knowledge that his mother will protect him—as long as the bond between you is firm."

Following this reasoning, even the mothers of teenagers who become violent at home are sometimes advised to hug their children like babies, in order to enable them to go back and reintegrate Erikson's stages of development.

It is important to note, however, that separation anxiety and stranger fear are limited to one period of life: they intensify at a certain age and then decline. The changes in intensity of separation anxiety with age are shown in figure 8-1. For a short time after birth, no separation anxiety exists. It then grows rapidly during the first year, reaches a peak around age two, falls to a lower level, and finally vanishes almost completely around the ages of four and a half to five. The significant thing about the age of two is that children are just learning to talk. And by five they have largely mastered language skills. Bower focused on the fact that each of these ages is a milestone in the development of the ability to communicate verbally.

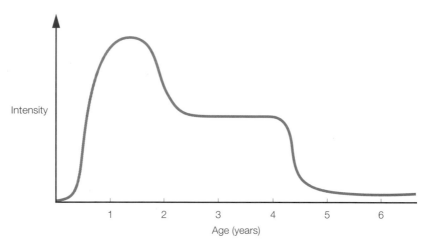

Fig. 8-1. The changes in intensity of separation anxiety with age

Source: Reprinted from T. G. R. Bower, *A Primer of Infant Development.*[5]

Speech could be called a form of general communication since it does not require a specific partner. Once children can talk, they can communicate with anyone who speaks the same language— they can even ask for directions from a passerby in the street. This may not seem surprising, but it is actually a remarkable achievement.

Before they acquire the language that makes this possible, however, infants pass through a stage of communication which is specific to a certain partner or partners, with whom they can make themselves understood by body language. For example, the baby's facial expression may tell its mother that it is wet or hungry. We could say that attachment is the state of being able to communicate in this way with particular individuals. Bower characterizes the attachment that forms between mother and infant as "a rich channel of communication—a form of nonverbal communication that is highly specific to these two human beings."

Viewing shyness and separation anxiety in this light, we could say that, to a baby, a person with whom it has not formed an attachment is like a speaker of a foreign language. Since many Japanese feel intimidated when asked directions in the street by an English-speaking foreigner, we might compare the child's fear of strangers to the alarm felt by adults in this situation, and separation anxiety to the fear a Japanese traveling overseas might feel on losing sight of his or her Japanese-speaking companions. But as one acquires language skills, speakers of that language, at least, cease to be so alarmingly foreign. Accordingly, stranger fear and separation anxiety disappear as the capacity for general communication develops. Bower concludes that this is the significance of the sudden decline of separation anxiety at ages two and five.

It follows that the best advice to give the mother of an excessively shy or clinging child is very different from the conventional wisdom cited earlier. This is the advice she should be getting: "The problem is that you've been keeping him too much to yourself. He hasn't had the contact with other children and adults that he needs in order to acquire more general communication skills. Don't keep him fenced in. For his own sake, push him out into other people's company. It may be a bit of a struggle, but children learn by experience to get along with other people."

Incidentally, in Japan, shopkeepers' children are often said to be less prone to shyness. According to the traditional Japanese practice, the mother carries the baby strapped on her back as she works in the shop, and thus the baby grows used to being spoken to by customers and learns quite naturally to interact with new people.

It might seem obvious that a child who is fearful of strangers needs to be given opportunities to grow accustomed to other people. Strangely, however, for years the experts gave exactly the opposite advice. As so often happens, their conceptual framework had obscured what should have been obvious. They seem to have assumed that every childhood problem stems from a weak mother-child relationship, an assumption based on the ideal of the modern family. If a child was clingy, it was due to a weak bond with the mother; if a child was perfectly happy away from its mother, this too was the fault of a weak bond. The experts had weak bonds on the brain. The resulting school of thought is known as maternal deprivation theory.

The advice given to mothers on the basis of such theories was surely counterproductive in many cases. A number of the developmental disorders seen in recent years are thought to be caused not by too much distance between mother and child but by too little,[6] and a great deal of harm may have been done in the course of advising all mothers who experienced such problems that they were insufficiently attached to their children.

Theories about human behavior and society exist not in a vacuum but against a background of particular social conditions. In Japan, as we saw in earlier chapters, barely twenty years elapsed between the establishment of the modern family system and the first throes of change in that system. Thus one can hardly blame those who went on automatically giving advice designed to help create the modern family, but it is time we recognized that this advice is now dangerously out of date.

THE CONDITIONS THAT PRODUCE ANXIOUS MOTHERS

There are, of course, contemporary studies of parent-child relationships which take into account the changing times. For example, over the last ten years Makino Katsuko has built up a body of research on what are known in Japan as "child-rearing neurosis" and "child-rearing anxiety."[7] She has concluded that, for the mother, establishing a certain degree of separation from her child is clearly linked to maintaining a healthier attitude to child rearing.

We have already looked at some issues that arise on the child's side of the relationship, in the form of developmental disorders. When parents become unable to act appropriately, the main phenomena which arise on their side of the relationship are child abuse and child-rearing neurosis.

Lately, my attention has been caught by ads on television for a child abuse hot line. When I first saw the slogan "This number is for you," I thought it must be advertising a hot line for reporting abuse in one's neighborhood, but in fact the majority of callers are people who have abused their own children—ordinary people who acted in the heat of the moment, and afterwards were distressed and unable to understand how they could have done such a thing.

At the root of child abuse is what is known in Japan as "child-rearing neurosis," which might be defined as a very severe form of child-rearing anxiety. In 1986, I was in charge of a research project on child-care support for nuclear families at the Hyogo Prefecture Domestic Problems Research Institute. During the one-year period of the study, in Hyogo Prefecture alone there were two cases in which a mother killed herself and her child due to child-rearing neurosis. Both families lived in similar locales, namely, new residential developments consisting of block after block of apartment towers.

Any mother can suffer from anxiety over the care of her child, though not necessarily to the point of neurosis. Makino defines child-rearing anxiety as "an emotional state including accumulated vague fears concerning one's child or the rearing of one's child." She uses the criteria shown in table 8-1 to determine whether this state exists in a particular instance.[8]

Although I was already aware that any mother can suffer such anxiety, I was nevertheless startled by the results of my interviews for the Hyogo study. All the leaders of mothers' clubs said the same thing: "To tell the truth, before I joined this group, I was in a pretty bad state. I had a kind of child-rearing neurosis." By the time I met these mothers, however, all appeared lively and active—a long way from a nervous breakdown.

Let me introduce the experience of one of them, a woman who is now brimming with vitality.[9] For some time after her marriage and the birth of her child, she lived near where she herself was born and grew up. She had friends in the neighborhood, and everything in her life was going well. Then her husband received a transfer and they moved to another prefecture. Many other transferees lived in the same area, and as this was just one of a series of short-term postings for all of them, they tended not to become close to their neighbors. The woman suddenly found herself isolated. At the same time her husband, being new at the office and anxious to make a good impression, began working late.

Left alone in the new house until late at night, she began to heap verbal abuse on her child at the slightest provocation. "It was no use screaming at the walls," she recalled, "and there was no

Table 8-1. Criteria and levels of child-rearing anxiety

Have you been feeling like this recently?

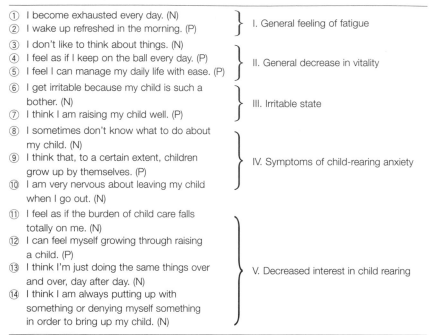

① I become exhausted every day. (N) ② I wake up refreshed in the morning. (P)	I. General feeling of fatigue
③ I don't like to think about things. (N) ④ I feel as if I keep on the ball every day. (P) ⑤ I feel I can manage my daily life with ease. (P)	II. General decrease in vitality
⑥ I get irritable because my child is such a bother. (N) ⑦ I think I am raising my child well. (P)	III. Irritable state
⑧ I sometimes don't know what to do about my child. (N) ⑨ I think that, to a certain extent, children grow up by themselves. (P) ⑩ I am very nervous about leaving my child when I go out. (N)	IV. Symptoms of child-rearing anxiety
⑪ I feel as if the burden of child care falls totally on me. (N) ⑫ I can feel myself growing through raising a child. (P) ⑬ I think I'm just doing the same things over and over, day after day. (N) ⑭ I think I am always putting up with something or denying myself something in order to bring up my child. (N)	V. Decreased interest in child rearing

Note: P = positive item, N = negative item.
Source: Compiled from Makino Katsuko, "A reexamination of the concept of 'child-rearing anxiety' and the factors which influence it."[8]

one else I could take my feelings out on." Around this time, an old friend happened to come for a visit. Her friend heard her tone of voice as she scolded the child and said, "This isn't like you. You never got so angry before." The comment brought her to her senses and made her realize that she couldn't go on in this way. "I've got to make friends," she thought. "If I can't find company around here, I'll take the bus to wherever I have to go." Locating the mothers' club solved this woman's problem; however, her story demonstrates how easily a normally happy person can be reduced to child-rearing neurosis. In this case the trigger was a move to another area, but it could be any number of factors, such as a dispute with neighbors.

Modern child rearing seems to be structured in a way that tends to promote anxiety. Makino's research points to two especially important structural factors.[10] The first is the lack of cooperation from the fathers. When a woman tries to talk to her husband about her problems with the children, the husband, who has come home tired from work, will often say, "Look, that's your department. Don't complain to me." Left to cope by herself, she is pushed further toward anxiety by his indifference.

The other major factor is the fact that mothers have very limited social networks of their own—and not just in connection with child rearing. A lack of help with child rearing can lead to neurosis in obvious ways, but studies also show the importance of contacts with other adults, whether or not these are related to children. Hobby groups are one example. Mothers are often told, "I don't see why you have to go to a hobby class while your child is so small." According to Makino's findings, however, mothers who attend such classes are clearly less prone to child-rearing anxiety.[11] Because they do not make their children their only purpose in life, and because they have somewhere to go for a change of pace, they feel refreshed when they come back to the children. In fact, it is while their children are small that mothers most need to create such time for themselves.

In the questionnaire results shown in figure 8-2, Makino found that most mothers in both the anxiety-prone and the anxi-

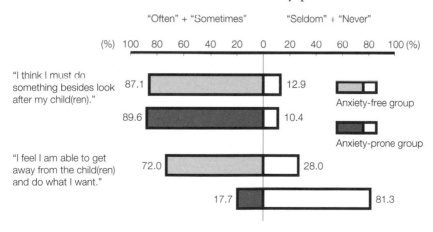

Fig. 8-2. Purposes in life besides child rearing

Source: Reprinted from Makino Katsuko, "The daily life and 'child-rearing anxiety' of mothers with infants."[7]

ety-free groups said they sometimes or often thought they must do something besides look after their children. All young mothers today feel this way, and perhaps older generations of postwar mothers felt this way, too. The crucial difference between the two groups in Makino's study lies in their answers to the second question. Those who said they sometimes or often felt they were able to get away and do what they wanted were generally free from child-rearing anxiety, whereas those who said they seldom or never felt this way were much more likely to be anxiety-prone.[12]

We see from these results that having some other interest in life helps prevent child-rearing anxiety. Thus, advising a woman to focus calmly on the care of her children and ignore her own self-realization will not serve the children. It is far better that she throw guilt to the winds and make time for herself. She will then be able to come back refreshed from her personal activity and be a better mother.

We have looked at two anxiety-inducing factors: the lack of fathers' cooperation, and mothers' limited social networks. These two factors can be equated with the sexual division of labor and the confinement of women to the domestic sphere, both results of the shift to the housewife role for women. All of a mother's energy—and all of her stress—has as its focus the one or two children who make up the smaller-sized family. Confined in the capsule of the home, both mother and child have lost the extended ties that were once available to them. The mother takes out her anxiety on the child, and the child, lacking the opportunity to develop social skills, remains dependent on the mother. The pathologies of the mother-child relationship so frequent in Japan today are bred through this mechanism of excessive closeness.

In the previous chapter, we found that the phenomenon of the housewife's malaise was brought about by two social conditions: the shift to the housewife role, and the smaller number of children per couple. The excessive closeness of mother and child can also be traced to the same pair of causes.

These conditions are two of the three characteristics I have attributed to the Postwar Family System. Thus, neither the housewife's malaise nor the excessive closeness of mother and child is a phenomenon of especially troubled families. They could have arisen in any family in postwar Japan, and perhaps every family has in fact experienced them in some latent form. One might say that, as a direct result of its structure, the Postwar Family System was destined to encounter these problems. Furthermore, as we saw in chapter 5, these two characteristics are in fact common to the twentieth-century modern family in the West. Thus, the housewife's malaise and the excessive closing-in of children can be seen as structural weaknesses of the modern family itself.

REORGANIZING CHILD-CARE NETWORKS

In this chapter, we have been looking at the frequently heard view that parents these days are bad parents. To determine whether this view is valid, we critically examined the theoretical framework which underlies it, and found that although pathologies associated with difficulties in child rearing have indeed become more common, they are due not to parental inadequacy, but to the structural weaknesses of the modern family. Then is there any way that parents today can escape this fate? To answer this question, I would like to consider what direction child care is likely to take in the future, using as clues some observations made in recent years.

One such clue is the different levels of child-care-related interaction among neighbors in urban and rural districts. Table 8-2 is based on a random sample of mothers in Hyogo Prefecture whose first child was aged two at the time of the survey, which I conducted in 1986.[13] In general, rural dwellers were found to associate more with their neighbors, as is popularly believed; however, with regard to support in caring for infants, more active neighborhood contacts were seen in the cities. The different trend is quite striking here, and similar findings have been reported in other areas.[14]

The reason for this difference becomes clear when we also consider family types, as shown in table 8-3.[15] In the rural districts covered by the survey, over 60 percent of the households with infants were extended family households. With grandparents living in the same house, there was enough help available without

Table 8-2. Regional differences in neighborhood contacts related to child rearing

	Almost daily	2 or 3 times a week	3 or 4 times a month	Almost never	Total
Urban areas	136	96	45	58	335
	(40.6)	(28.7)	(13.4)	(17.3)	(100)
Rural areas	27	42	38	48	155
	(17.4)	(27.1)	(24.5)	(31.0)	(100)

Note: Figures in parentheses are percentages.
Source: Reprinted from Hyogo-ken Katei Mondai Kenkyujo, "Report on a study of child-care support for nuclear families."[9]

Table 8-3. Regional differences in family type

	Living with husband's parents	Living with wife's parents	Living next door to husband's parents	Living next door to wife's parents	Living near husband's parents	Living near wife's parents	Isolated nuclear family	Total
Urban areas	67	12	32	23	62	23	116	335
	(20.0)	(3.6)	(9.6)	(6.9)	(18.5)	(6.9)	(34.5)	(100)
Rural areas	83	17	13	7	15	9	10	154
	(54.1)	(11.0)	(8.4)	(4.5)	(9.7)	(5.8)	(6.5)	(100)

Note: Figures in parentheses are percentages.
Source: Reprinted from Hyogo-ken Katei Mondai Kenkyujo, "Report on a study of child-care support for nuclear families."[9]

making a special effort to contact other mothers in the neighborhood. In contrast, 35 percent of urban families are isolated nuclear families, which were defined in this study as nuclear families located at least 40 minutes' traveling time away from the residences of both sets of grandparents. When asked how they came to know the people they associated with in the neighborhood, in rural areas nearly 50 percent replied "We knew each other before our children were born." In urban areas, close to 30 percent said they had intentionally sought contact because they wanted playmates for their children. Thus, the thriving child-care networks in urban areas today are a new kind of community, as it were, deliberately created by parents under the pressure of necessity.

In chapter 4, we discussed the sibling networks of the sixties family. Studies done at the time provided evidence that kin networks and neighborhood networks were interchangeable, even then. However, those who were of child-rearing age in the 1960s were members of the transitional generation in demographic terms, and as such they had many siblings. Since many of these women, even in urban areas, could call on their sisters for help, in practice they did not develop strong neighborhood communities.

When we compare the network situation in the 1960s and the 1980s, the observed changes fit the theoretical predictions remarkably well. By the 1980s child rearing had shifted mainly to the post-transitional generation, who are poor in siblings; hence urban families, having almost completely lost their kin networks, were forced to develop neighborhood networks instead.

Thus, during the two stable decades of the Postwar Family System, while it is true that Japanese families fit the global model of the modern family, at the same time Japan's demographic conditions made available the sibling networks which protected them from isolation and fragility, the modern family's weak points. When these protective conditions were gone, the Japanese family was laid bare as a stereotypical modern family. That may be one reason why various problems first surfaced in the latter half of the 1970s.

Mothers and their children have not been passive, however. They have been resourceful enough to create the social networks they needed, like the woman in the example of child-rearing neurosis who joined a group because she couldn't go on as she was. The development of urban neighborhood networks in the 1980s was a result of the resilience of mothers who had been driven into a corner. Out of their groping efforts, a new mode of child care was spontaneously generated for the new era.

Actually, even where a child's grandparents live in the same house, a network is still needed, since playing with an adult in attendance is no substitute for having friends. Adults may say "Don't do that!" but only another child says "That's mine!" Unless children have the experience of repeatedly asserting themselves, being made to wait, and so on, among other children who are just as stubborn as they are, they do not learn to build equal relationships.

One kindergarten was prompted to begin a class for two-year-olds in light of what happened when children about to be enrolled at the usual age of three were brought together to play. The children, sitting in a circle, were supposed to roll a ball back and forth, but each child kept hold of it. They were incapable of passing the ball on. Since they had always played with adults, they were unable to understand such things as sharing toys and taking turns with other children.[16]

Such stories only confirm what an impossible task it is to bring up children in isolation. Just as parents need peers of their own, children need someone of their own age to play with. Because of the declining birthrate, however, in some places there are hardly any children to be found. This is true not only in rural communities which have been losing their young adult population through migration, but even in the cities—in expensive residential suburbs, for example. Some parents are actually having so much difficulty finding playmates for their children that they drive them every day to parks in distant areas where there are more youngsters.[17] As this shows, it often takes deliberate effort to make and maintain social contacts with other parents and children.

Obviously, then, not all needs can be met by the spontaneous activity of neighborhood networks. Indeed, the mothers' club which the woman in my example joined had been brought together by a child-rearing course set up by the local government. When we speak of government support for child care, we may imagine the government taking responsibility for every aspect, but in fact more limited measures can often provide adequate support. For example, community centers and children's centers can provide opportunities and facilities for those who wish to form their own networks. The telephone counseling services for parents which have already been launched all over the country are another effective means of support. Yet another possibility would be to introduce a more open enrollment policy at public day-care centers and kindergartens, many of which have vacancies due to the smaller number of infants. At present it is not possible to enroll a child in public day care for the express reason of providing him or her with playmates; perhaps the regulations need to be updated.

According to Philippe Ariès, "[the] overexpansion of the family role is a result of the decline of the city and of the urban forms of social intercourse that it provided. . . . The real roots of the present domestic crisis lie not in our families, but in our cities."[18]

At no time in history has the group known as "the family" raised children unaided. Children have always grown up surrounded by various networks—neighborhood women, uncles and cousins, playmates, schoolmates, and many others. The reason why today's parents appear to be in difficulties is that the networks concerned with children's growth are undergoing change, and this reorganization is not going smoothly. If they cannot turn to relatives, they turn to the local community. If they cannot find enough help there, they look to public support. By combining all of these resources in flexible ways, they are attempting to arrive at a new mode of child care suited to the conditions of contemporary society.

THE MEANING OF HAVING CHILDREN

During the 1970s and 1980s, the contradictions inherent in the Postwar Family System all erupted at once. These problems arose not because the ideal of the postwar family was unrealizable, but precisely because it had been realized. It is truly ironic—though not altogether uncommon—that as soon as people think they have achieved their ideal, its unforeseen ill effects begin to appear.

Perhaps it was actually in attempting to escape the grip of these problems, which were regarded as a crisis and a breakdown, that the family unwittingly took its first steps toward a new transformation.

As I have mentioned a number of times, structural change in the Postwar Family System first showed up statistically in about 1975. In the previous chapter I discussed in detail how the first characteristic of the system, the shift to the housewife's role for women, came to be reversed. As for the second characteristic, reproductive egalitarianism, from 1975 onward the second decrease in the birthrate clearly indicated that a change was in the making, and the consternation of the government and the media when the total fertility rate reached 1.57 and then 1.53 is still a very recent memory.

As I explained at the end of chapter 3, the fertility rate can be considered to equal the product of the marriage rate and the marital fertility rate. Within the range of observations to date, the change which has occurred in these variables since 1975 consists entirely of a decline in the marriage rate. People's reproductive behavior once they marry has remained unchanged. In this respect, the second decline in fertility is completely unlike the first, seen during the 1950s.

The present decline in the marriage rate is mainly due to later marriages. In the eyes of those who are concerned about a dwindling population, the Hanakos are to blame. Although opinion polls have not found a marked increase in the number of people choosing to remain single, demographers nevertheless predict that the trend toward later marriage will lead to increasing percentages of men and women remaining single all their lives. And when the late-marrying Hanako generation have finished bearing children, the rate of marital fertility may show a new decline, reflecting in part the influence of those who, having started families at a late age, did not try to have more than one child.

At least with regard to marriage and childbirth, a greater diversity of lifestyles is likely to emerge as people make different choices at different points in time: whether or not to marry, and if so, whether to do it earlier or later; whether or not to have children, and if so, whether to have one, two, or three. In other words, reproductive egalitarianism will become a thing of the past.

With the end of the system in which everyone was expected to marry and create a modern family with two or three children, what sort of changes can we expect to see in the parent-child relationship? Already, we are seeing the first signs of weakening of the idea that a family is not a family without children, and of the belief that being born into the human race carries with it the duty to become a parent in one's turn. If parents no longer raise children out of a sense of duty or compulsion, perhaps the parent-child relationship may become less claustrophobic.

But such a transformation also means that children become true "consumer durables." Having children becomes an option in the same category as buying a car or taking a trip. The Hanako generation does indeed seem to have adopted a mentality consistent with this new era. They have evidently decided that they will love and enjoy those children they do have to the full—but if there's no pleasure in it, they're not interested in having children at all.

Before criticizing the Hanakos, however, we should ask ourselves whether we can explain why anyone should have children—not in terms of the labor force and the aging of society, which are concerns of the state, but in the words of individuals living their day-to-day lives.

In years to come, the question of why people have children will inevitably become more of a mystery. If they no longer do so because children are economic assets (as in the days when they were producer goods), nor because everybody else has them (the norm of the modern family), then, in return for their new freedom, people will have to discover their own reasons for having children. In the end, it will probably come down to enjoyment (children as consumer durables), or, to put it more seriously, because bringing up children provides one with an irreplaceable part of the human experience. But what if, having had a child, it turns out to provide more pain than pleasure? What if, as the child grows older and less cute, it becomes less enjoyable? Unlike cars and video games, there is no market for secondhand children.

At present, the necessity to produce children is felt with true urgency not by the family, let alone by the individual; it is felt only by the state, which is anxious to secure labor resources for the future. There would in fact be no further worry on this score if labor were allowed to move freely across national borders, but to allow this would call into question the very basis of existence of the nation-state. Such considerations are behind the great commotion that the government and media are making over the falling fertility rate.

It should be noted that the decline in birth and marriage rates is not confined to Japan alone. Similar declines are also being seen in the developed nations of the West, and some demographers are calling this a second demographic transition—a point to which we will return in chapter 10. The observed trends give rise to a host of questions. Where are these changes leading? Are there national or regional differences? How are the trends in the developed nations related to population growth in the Third World? How are they related to the ecosystem? What part is being played by the development of reproductive technologies? How long will the nation-state remain viable? Faced with so many momentous questions, we may begin to imagine the kind of answers found in science fiction, but we cannot see far enough into the future to know with any certainty. The new structure has yet to reveal itself completely.

Chapter 9 | # Bilaterality and the Future of the *Ie*

THE THIRD GENERATION FORMS FAMILIES

In this chapter we turn to a subject which arouses more strong feelings than any other among people of all ages in Japan: the future of the *ie* system and the care of elderly parents.

Recently, a former student of mine came to see me on campus. "I'm thinking of getting married," she told me, "but I'm a little worried." When I asked what was the matter, she explained that she was the elder of two sisters and her fiancé was an eldest son. They had been close to setting a wedding date when he presented her with the following scenario: "What if, in the future, our parents get sick at the same time? Even you couldn't manage to look after both yours and mine," he had said. "So if it comes to that, you'll have to put yours in an old folks' home." Incredible as it may seem to Western readers, he was insisting on this as a condition of the marriage—a condition which the young woman could not readily accept. But in Japan, while not exactly commonplace, such a condition for marriage is quite conceivable.

As we saw in chapter 7, in the 1980s the phrase "women's independence" was a keynote of change in the family. A less visible undercurrent, however, was the reemergence of problems relating to the *ie*, which had already seemed a thing of the past. Today, these problems have taken on such proportions that they may, in fact, be the most important family issues the Japanese will face in the 1990s and on into the early years of the twenty-first century.

The year 1975, which marked the end of the stable period of the Postwar Family System, was a turning point in many ways. As the impact of the 1973 oil crisis subsided, the Japanese economy entered on a new phase of moderate growth. Nineteen seventy-five was also International Women's Year and the start of the United Nations Decade of Women. As it happened, it was during that very decade that Japanese women moved away from the house-wife's role and began changing their lives. It was also at this time that reproductive egalitarianism began to break down.

From a demographic viewpoint, it was in the mid-1970s that the third generation, in which both the birthrate and infant mortality had reached their post-transitional low levels, began to marry and form families. As you may recall, the demographic third generation was born after about 1950; thus, if the average age at marriage was 25, they began to marry around 1975. And it was after this point that problems stemming from the demographic conditions of the third generation began to emerge. This generation (to which I myself belong) is characterized chiefly by having a small number of siblings. As its members have formed families, their experience has inevitably been different from that of the second generation, which was most active in starting families during the 1960s, when the Postwar Family System was at its height. Thus, whether we like it or not, change has already been under way for some time now.

In chapters 6, 7, and 8, we focused on changes in the first and second characteristics of the Postwar Family System. These changes concerned aspects of the system—women's role and the number of children per couple—which are common to the modern family in general. In this chapter, we will look finally at how Japanese families are likely to change in order to accommodate the characteristics of the third generation, or, in other words, to adapt to the loss of those demographic conditions which have supported the features of the family that are specific to Japan.

THE NUCLEARIZATION OF THE FAMILY REACHES ITS LIMITS

First, it may be useful to briefly review what we discussed in chapters 4 and 5. We discovered that the Postwar Family System existed under demographically unique conditions; that is to say, during the period when this system was stable, most of the families formed were those of the demographic second generation, a large population with many siblings. As a result, it was possible for the norm of the traditional *ie* system—household successors living with their parents—to coexist alongside the nuclearization of the family. Further, because they were supported by sibling networks, families appeared to have a high degree of self-sufficiency.

Now let us see how changing demographic conditions have affected the family since 1975. The first consequence was that the nuclearization of the family reached its limits. Apparently there is a widespread impression, often restated in the press, that the nuclearization of the family is still progressing. This is, however, a complete myth. As figure 4-1 clearly shows, the ratio of nuclear family households has leveled off and even declined since 1975. The reasons are fairly obvious: first, there has been an increase in one-person households, and second, 1975 was the turning point in the transition from the era of the second generation to that of the third. Where parents in the second generation typically had four children, those in the third generation have two. Thus, there are no longer any "spares," since the children of the third generation are typically either successors themselves or will marry successors. If the norm of co-residence of stem family successors with their parents were strictly observed, no nuclear families would be generated when the children in this generation married.

Due to individual circumstances, however, not all children who might be expected to live with their parents are able or willing to do so. As a result, the percentage of parents who live with their children is decreasing (figure 9-1). Thus we see a phenomenon which is often cited as a social problem, the increase in households consisting of elderly couples or one elderly person living alone. In terms of the percentage of children who live with

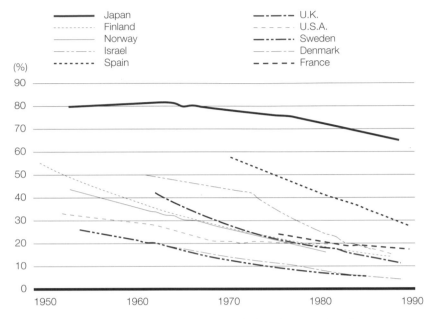

Fig. 9-1. The declining percentage of elderly people who co-reside with their children

Note: For each country, figures represent the ratio to the total population of persons aged 65 years and over, with the following exceptions: Norway, 1953, and Sweden, 1954: persons aged 67 years and over. France, 1990: persons aged 60 years and over. Denmark, all years: persons aged 70 years and over . *Sources*: Based on Gerdt Sundström, "Care by Families," in OECD, *Caring for Frail Elderly People* (Chapter 2).

their parents, however, according to a study by Hiroshima Kiyoshi, between 1975 and 1985 there was actually a slight increase in co-residence by children in their twenties and thirties, reflecting the drop in the number of siblings; since then, the rate has been declining.[1]

Reports of the growing number of old people living alone may give the impression that the third generation is coldhearted, but, on the contrary, given that we belong to a much smaller sibling pool, it would be especially hard for individual members of our generation to distance ourselves from our parents, even if we wanted to.

In the late 1980s, there was a hit TV series titled *Danjo shichinin natsumonogatari* (A summer tale of seven men and women) and its sequel, *Danjo shichinin akimonogatari* (An autumn tale of seven men and women). These were early examples of a new genre known as the "trendy drama." The story revolved around the romance of a couple who were about my age, and both very anxious to have their partner make a good impression on their parents. I had to smile wryly at the accuracy of this picture. For baby boomers, who have more siblings, it might have been possible to go ahead with a marriage against parental opposition, even if it meant they never spoke to their parents again, but things are not so simple for the third generation.[2]

THE TRAGEDY OF THE DAUGHTER WHO IS EXPECTED TO SUCCEED

By pointing to the persistence of *ie*-related problems, I do not mean to raise the specter of the *ie* system coming back to life, because in reality I think we are moving in quite the opposite direction. In discussing the nuclearization of the family, I pointed out that, although it was often said to have died out after the war, the system which places great importance on the continuity of the household line had remained in existence. But now I am going to predict the demise of the *ie* system. Though it will not be proclaimed in headlines as it was after the war, we have now come to the point where, for demographic reasons, the *ie* system will be forced to undergo a transformation, if not disappear altogether.

For argument's sake, let us say that the *ie* system is basically patrilineal. (Actually, although it is commonly given this label, the Japanese system is not purely patrilineal. If it were, the line would die out when there is no direct male heir, but in the absence of a son, a daughter's husband has traditionally been adopted as the household successor. We will return to this point later.)

Once we assume patrilineal descent, it becomes a question of simple arithmetic. The typical family has two children. Let us suppose that each family follows a purely patrilineal system, that is, the successor must be a son, while a daughter marries into another family. If there are two sons, one (probably the younger) may leave home, as long as the other remains. Families with two daughters will cease to exist as *ie*. The ratio of families that will cease to exist can then be calculated as follows. Since there are four possible permutations and combinations of two children (boy-boy, boy-girl, girl-boy, girl-girl), one in four households will have two girls. In an *ie* system run according to a strictly patrilineal principle, fully one in four *ie* would die out in each generation.[3] One in four couples could not look to their children for support in their old age, and one in four graves would be left untended by any descendants.

I have used a simplified formula here to demonstrate where *ie*-oriented thinking leads in the age of two-child families. But those who come from all-girl families in Japan, and their parents, should take heed: unless there is a change in this orientation, an unhappy fate awaits them. Many of my women friends, being the only child or the eldest in a family of girls, are unable to marry because their parents have hopes of their finding a husband who will agree to be legally adopted, thus taking the wife's family name. Even if a woman in this position falls in love, three out of four men are eldest sons with obligations of their own, and (unless her family has a very sizable fortune) any talk of marriage will soon reach an impasse. Quite a few couples I know have been prevented from marrying for two or three years, solely because of this problem of the family name.

In most cases, the woman reluctantly gives up her name to solve this impasse. But then she faces a new set of demands from her mother-in-law. "You're taking off to see your parents far too often. You're a member of the X family now, and it's time you stopped expecting your parents to pamper you. Now when I was newly married. . ." But the situation is completely different from when her mother-in-law married: unlike the second generation with its many siblings, the young wife today has no brother at home to whom she can confidently leave the care of her parents. If she doesn't keep an eye on them, no one else will.

And then there is the matter of the family graves. Today, a growing number of temples will allow a married daughter to take financial responsibility for the upkeep of her own family's graves. But if a married woman wants to fulfill all the observances for relatives on both her own and her husband's side, she will be kept busy year-round attending the memorial services which are held on certain anniversaries of a person's death. She could also find herself having to make room for two Buddhist family altars in one small apartment, and to rush about the country from one family's graves to the other's at Obon and Ohigan, the times of year (in midsummer and at the spring and autumn equinoxes) when the Japanese traditionally honor their ancestors.

ADOPTED SONS AND SEPARATE FAMILY NAMES

We noted earlier that the *ie* in Japan is not a purely patrilineal system. In fact, the flexibility that makes possible adoption of a successor has been extremely important in maintaining the *ie* system under variable demographic conditions.[4] When we go back beyond the second generation to the first, the high infant and child mortality rate coupled with a high birthrate meant that the number of children who reached adulthood was almost the same as the number in the third generation. The active adoption of successors was the key to the survival of the *ie* system under these conditions, with very few *ie* being allowed to die out. Going even further back in time, historical demographic studies have determined that, at the end of the Edo Period, about 20 percent of all heads of household in the peasant class were adopted sons.[5] The ratio appears to have been highest in the warrior class.[6] To younger sons in this period, being adopted into another household to become its successor was a perfectly obvious life choice.

After World War II, however, the number of such adoptions declined.[7] This resulted not from democratization, but from the fact that adoption was seldom necessary in the sibling-rich second generation. The upshot was that people grew accustomed to a new situation in which men's surnames did not change. One could say that the *ie* became a more nearly pure patrilineal system after the Second World War.

Now that Japan's demographic conditions have returned to approximately those of the first generation, can we expect men to go back to changing their names without hesitation? If so, the *ie* system will be on safe ground; if not, one in four household lines are doomed. There does seem to have been a slight increase in son-in-law adoptions,[8] but the level remains far below the 20 percent documented in the Edo Period. In an era when they no longer have to take over a family business but can make their way as company employees, there are probably few men willing to be dominated by their wives' parents. Thus, the tragic plight of the daughter who is expected to succeed is not yet over.

This brings us to a subject which has been much in the news lately: the proposed revision of the Civil Code to allow spouses to retain separate family names. Even now, some married women do continue to use their old names informally, but the proposed legislation would allow them to do this officially. There are two groups lobbying for this reform: working women whose careers are disrupted by a name change, and parents of all-girl families.

However, the relationship between the proposed system and the traditional *ie* is far from straightforward. Although the parents of daughters are motivated by the desire to preserve their family name and household continuity, the introduction of separate surnames would lead to a major transformation of the *ie* system, if not its demise. For there is another aspect of the *ie* system which is just as important as the continuity of the line, and that is the group identity of the *ie*. Individuals traditionally belonged to only one *ie*, and were loyal to it as an organization. In principle, at least, an individual cannot be a member of two *ie* at once. There is a very familiar scene in TV dramas in which the parents of a young bride-to-be tell her, gently but firmly, "You're no longer a member of this *ie*, so no matter what happens, don't think you can come back home." The spirit of group identity embodied in the *ie* system does not permit divided loyalties. But this principle would collapse once spouses began using different surnames. In practice, the couple would tend to associate more or less equally with both sets of parents and other relatives.

In fact, there are signs that this change is already under way, even without reform of the Civil Code. These days, in real life, parents tell their daughters, "Even though you're getting married, this will always be your home. You can come back any time if it doesn't work out." Also, the word *jikka*, traditionally used to refer to a married woman's parental home, has recently come to be widely used in reference to the husband's parental home as well—and not only in those few cases where he has been adopted into his wife's *ie*. This, too, could be taken to signify that the couple's relationship with their two families of origin has become more symmetrical.

WHAT IS BILATERALITY?

"Bilaterality" is an anthropological term for one type of kinship structure. Bilaterality has been the subject of much debate. Since the nineteenth century, anthropologists have been aware of the existence of societies in which the inheritance of a family name, status, and property was structured by a patrilineal principle (passing, that is, from father to son), or by a matrilineal principle (passing from mother to daughter). Controversy arose, however, when it was suggested that some societies did not seem to fit either of these schemes. The debate revolved around whether such societies were neither patrilineal nor matrilineal, or were both simultaneously ("bilineal"), or were simply flexible according to circumstances ("optional"). In the final analysis, it seems best to consider that such societies form kinship relations which are structured more by the relative closeness or distance of relationships between individuals than by a particular genealogical principle.

Southeast Asia is one region known to have a distinct bilateral system. This has been attributed to the development of agricultural methods which were adapted to the flood cycle of the region's rivers—rivers too large for human control—and which consequently did not require social organization for the management of water resources. Households in many parts of Southeast Asia have a nuclear family structure, but may be located either near the wife's or near the husband's parental home, depending on various circumstances. They also tend to have well-developed kin networks. Further, these nuclear family groups are not particularly cohesive; essentially, the individual comes first. Divorce rates are quite high, and the children of divorced parents are readily cared for by members of the kin network.[9]

East Asian societies, in contrast, are strongly patrilineal. However, Japan's close historical ties with Southeast Asia have led some scholars to argue that descent in ancient Japan was also bilateral. The pioneering historian and feminist Takamure Itsue theorized that Japan was originally a matrilineal society, but in light of more recent anthropological knowledge, bilaterality now has many advocates. Perhaps the flexible adoption practices seen in Japan can best be explained by a tradition of bilateral descent.

Whether ancient Japan was bilateral, patrilineal, or matrilineal is still open to debate, and we need not pursue this question further here. More importantly for our purposes, the concept of a shift to bilaterality may help us understand the changes that are overtaking kin relations in present-day Japan, as seen, for example, in the current controversy over separate surnames and worries over the upkeep of family graves.

It has been pointed out that, in Western societies, kin relations in the modern urban family have become bilateral.[10] However, it should be noted that families in most parts of preindustrial Northwestern Europe and America were already nuclear and relatively unconcerned with lineage.[11] To date, little research has been done on how the demographic transition affects the family system in a society such as Japan, with its non-Western cultural tradition in which the stem family is the norm.[12] It is hardly surprising that this question has received little attention until now, as related problems have only recently made themselves felt even in Japan, which modernized earliest among non-Western nations.

In suggesting that what we are experiencing could be called a shift to bilaterality, I am not merely taking an academic interest in nomenclature. In times of change, we need to decide whether the principles that operated in the past are still valid, and if they are not, to set about finding principles fit for the new era. And the first step in rethinking one's approach is to identify and name the changes that are occurring. Hence, "the shift to bilaterality."

Let us return to the case with which we began this chapter—the woman whose fiancé insisted her parents would have to be placed in a home. The old approach would have been for her to resign herself to the idea that she would really have no choice once she married into his family. She would simply talk herself into going along with his wishes. But as we have seen, this thinking requires that one in four elderly couples be abandoned by their children—not a very practical solution. As long as very few families were in this position, they were forced to accept it as their personal misfortune, while the system itself remained unchanged. But when one family in four is affected, a major upheaval may not be far off. If the existing system's days are numbered, it makes better sense for the young woman in this case to search for a new solution. She should search as if the future of the family in Japan depended on it. And if her fiancé proves too conservative to join her in finding a new approach, she does not have to join him in the old one.

In reality, a quiet revolution is already under way. We have seen that parents these days send off their daughters with assurances that they can always come home. In other ways, too, the parents of daughters are not admitting defeat. Little by little, they are changing their tactics. For example, regardless of whether or not their daughter keeps their family name, they may encourage her to live close to them, perhaps by buying her a house nearby or rebuilding on their own property to accommodate both households. Family surveys conducted by the Mainichi Newspapers Population Problems Research Council have shown that, although the total percentage of newly married couples co-residing with parents did not change greatly between 1981 and 1990, the percentage living with the wife's parents rose during this decade from 6.0 to 10.6 percent, while the percentage living with the husband's parents declined by a similar margin, from 34.8 to 28.2 percent.[13] Indeed, in the future it may be prospective bridegrooms and their parents who suffer if they do not change their way of thinking.

In any case, newlyweds today are caught in an undeclared tug-of-war between their two sets of parents. But all parties should take note that, for the reasons we have seen, young married couples today are unable to become full members of one *ie* or the other. They have to maintain a skillfully balanced relationship with both spouses' parents. This is the demographic fate of the younger generation today. A misguided attempt to absorb the couple completely into either *ie* will have tragic consequences, perhaps even precipitating a divorce. The age of bilaterality has already dawned.

LIVING TOGETHER, LIVING APART, LIVING NEARBY

In the age of bilaterality, whether or not they share the same address, the living arrangements that members of the third generation make in relation to their parents are inevitably very different from those of the second generation in the 1960s. At that time, eldest sons (or other successors) lived with the parents as a matter of course. It would not have occurred to them to have separate kitchens, as is often done today; they shared everything completely. Meanwhile, the younger sons and the daughters left home completely. What this meant in practice was that it was considered admirable if they visited their parents twice yearly, at Obon and New Year's. And if they could only manage to visit once a year, or even once in several years, that was good enough.

Thus, in the 1960s, children had very different relationships with their parents depending on whether or not they were successors, and hence whether or not they resided in the same household. Today, adult children still tend to think that their relationship with their parents hinges on whether or not they live together. But the truth is that, no matter which choice they make, the relationships that evolve in the future will not be the same as in the past.

The main difference is that hardly anyone has an elder brother they can count on to stay home and take care of their parents. As we noted earlier, three-fourths of the men of the third generation *are* the eldest son, and most women who marry will marry an eldest son. In the sixties, the other siblings were able to leave home with a clear conscience because one brother always stayed. Married daughters and younger sons who moved to the city could feel secure in the knowledge that he was there.

Today, however, one in every two children is what would once have been called a successor. With the waning of the value system which gave the successor special rights and duties, he too is more likely to leave his parents' home in response to job or housing conditions. Today, no children have the special inheritance privileges once reserved for the successor, but the trade-off is that no children have the "privilege" of not having to be concerned about their parents' welfare. And each has fewer siblings with whom to share those concerns.

A couple living with either the husband's or the wife's parents will feel obliged to phone and visit the other's parents regularly. Even if a couple live in their own separate household, they will not feel free to distance themselves completely from either spouse's parents. In this way, we can see a new bilateral relationship beginning to take shape.

Social scientists have predicted the upper and lower limits of the range in which the declining ratio of nuclear family households will one day stabilize.[14] Both they and the government are currently becoming very nervous as to just where in this range the actual figure will fall, because this will determine the number of people who will live alone in their old age. However, their anxiety seems somewhat misdirected if, as I foresee, the distinction between co-residing and non-co-residing families ceases to have the very real significance it has had until now.

As with many other practices in Japan, comparative cultural theories have been put forward to explain the attitude towards co-residence. Specifically, it has been pointed out that in Japan, a move away from the parental home tends to be to a distant city, whereas in the United States, adult children often live within easy visiting distance of their parents.[15] But even this apparent cultural difference may itself be largely explained by the simple fact that nonsuccessors could move far away without worrying as long as there was one sibling living at home with their parents. We know that, in future, the situation in Japan will come to resemble that in the United States more closely, in that there will be an increased number of parental households without co-residing children. When this happens, living at an intermediate distance, neither too near nor too far, may come to be viewed as the ideal in Japan.

At present, in Japan, adult children who live apart from their parents do not visit as often as their American counterparts do, and their visits are even rarer if one of their siblings is co-residing (figure 9-2). It seems there will also have to be a change in the attitude that adult children who leave the parental home have no responsibility for their parents.

Compared to the all-or-nothing arrangements of the past, whether they like it or not, parents and adult children will be making a wider variety of choices from now on as they work out new ways of associating with one another once the children marry. The recent interest in dual-household dwellings with separate entrances and kitchens is one tentative move in this direction.

The key is balancing the two sides of the family—from how often each gets to see the grandchildren, to how often each visits or extends an invitation. One frequently hears people say that just thinking about whose parents they are going to spend New Year's with makes them dread the approaching holiday. Their parents are probably just as perplexed. In the absence of established rules,

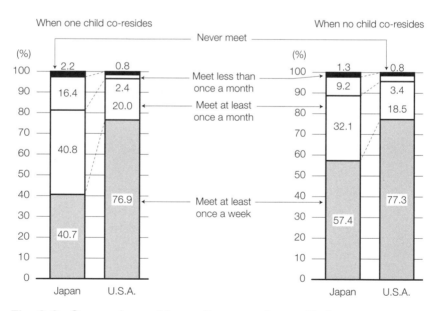

Fig. 9-2. Comparison of how often parents see their non-co-residing children, in Japan and the U.S.A.

Sources: Data for Japan from Tokyo Metropolitan Institute of Gerontology and University of Michigan, *Zenkoku koreisha chosa* (National survey of the elderly) (Tokyo, 1987); data for the U.S.A. from Institute for Social Research, University of Michigan, *Americans' Changing Lives: Wave I*, 1986.

Japanese families, both parents and children, are likely to go through a stressful period for some time to come.

NETWORKS IN THE AGING SOCIETY

Taking our cue from the fact that the nuclearization of the family has leveled off, we have seen that the *ie* system, which was able to exist compatibly alongside the nuclearization of the family in the 1960s, has now reached a point where fundamental change is inevitable.

In addition to the coexistence of the *ie* with nuclearization of the family, in chapter 4 we discussed a second consequence of the demographic transition as a characteristic of the Postwar Family System, namely, the importance of sibling networks. Exploring this question further in chapter 8, we found that families in the third generation were stripped down to the modern family proper, since they lacked the sibling networks which, in the second generation, had quietly provided support for child care. As a result, the pathologies of the modern family, that is, the isolation and excessive closeness of mother and child, have come to light. At the same time, however, families of the third generation have been resilient enough to begin organizing new social networks. Parents in urban areas are actively utilizing neighborhood networks, and are also calling for the provision of public and other forms of support.

Let us now take another look at the subject of networks, this time in relation to the aging of the population, which is generally considered the most important of the family-related issues of the future.

First, I would like to clear up a common misunderstanding with respect to the aging of Japanese society. Although many commentators link this phenomenon with the decline in fertility observed in recent years, it should be emphasized that the two are essentially unrelated. As we have seen, the oft-cited decline in the birthrate began around 1975. Long before that time, however, Japanese society was already destined to undergo rapid aging of its population. The root cause of this aging was the first drop in the birthrate from 1950 to 1958, in other words, the fertility transition. When the populations of the three demographic generations reached a ratio of 1:2:2, the die was cast. The ratio of the elderly population to the younger generation who would look after them was certain to rise rapidly from 1:2 to 2:2. It is nonsense to blame the late-marrying Hanako generation for the aging of society, or to think that it can be prevented if each woman has a few more babies. If there is any blame to be assigned, it is for the failure to take early measures to address this entirely predictable outcome.

If we define the elderly as persons aged 65 years and over, at present the majority of this group are members of the first generation. But the second generation (born between 1925 and 1950) have been rapidly adding to their numbers since 1990. The transition from 1:2 to 2:2 is taking place at this very moment (figure 9-3).

There is a Japanese expression meaning "passing the buck," which is often used derisively to describe siblings trying to force responsibility for their aging parents onto one another. These sib-

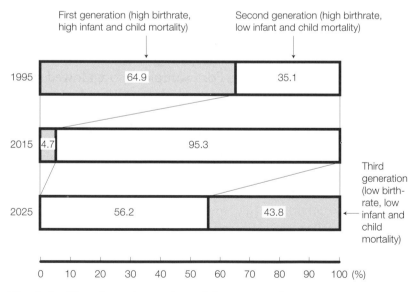

Fig. 9-3. The changing ratios of the generations among the elderly

Note: Figures are the ratios of the population of each generation to the total population aged 65 years and over.

Source: Data from Institute of Population Problems, Ministry of Health and Welfare, *Nihon no shorai jinko suikei* (Future population projections for Japan), estimates as of September 1992.

lings may actually be luckier than they know in having someone to pass the buck to. Their behavior could also be viewed in a more favorable light, as the mutual supportiveness of a sibling network. But when the many siblings of the second generation grow old, there will be no escape for their third-generation children. It is not inconceivable that some may even be driven to literally abandon their parents. Not long ago, there was news of an actual incident like this in the United States. A man suffering from senile dementia was left in his wheelchair in a crowded public place—by his own daughter, as it turned out. Watching her hide her face from the TV cameras as she fled the reporters without a word, one could only wonder what her life must have been like up to that point. Now that the time for addressing these issues has finally arrived in Japan, it is no use pining for something called "Japanese culture" that we have lost. Rather, what is needed is objective recognition of the changed conditions and concrete measures to adapt to them.

While the third generation may have nowhere to "pass the buck," we should bear in mind that they too are benefitting from the sibling networks of their elders. Being unable to rely on the support of their children, the second generation have already begun to support one another. For example, two widowed sisters who have not spent time together in a long while may suddenly decide to take a trip together, then they may begin to accompany each other on visits to the doctor, and when one is confined to bed the other may bring her meals. In such ways, the women who migrated in large numbers to the cities after the war are now reactivating the networks which played such an important role in raising their children, but this time it is for their own support. The third generation is also being helped immeasurably by the dependable presence of these aunts.

The situation will become truly serious when the third generation begins to age. With so few siblings, and no guarantee that they can rely on their children, what are they to do? As in the case of child care, if they cannot turn to kin networks, there are networks of neighbors and friends, and if these are not enough, they will have to create some other kind of network. The third generation probably has no alternative but to begin, well in advance, to prepare networks of their own to support their old age. Part of this preparation, of course, will be to ensure that adequate services are provided by both the public and private sectors.

THE AGE OF DOMESTIC LABOR SHORTAGE

Finally, let us examine an issue on a macro scale, namely, the labor shortage, from the point of view of the family.[16]

The third generation is now becoming the mainstay of Japanese society; what this means, in principle, is that we have entered an age of labor shortage. In contrast, during the 1960s, at the height of the rapid economic growth which was supported by the second generation, there were more than enough people to meet the demand for labor. The stable period of the Postwar Family System was a time of latent labor surplus.

When one views various aspects of Japanese society during the high-growth era in terms of population surplus, one makes some interesting discoveries. Take "Japanese-style management." The lifetime employment and seniority system which go under this name are usually explained in terms of Japanese groupism, but they can also be seen as an adaptation to conditions of labor surplus on the part of both companies and their workforces. Japanese-style management does not necessarily promote efficiency, since it is not a merit-based system. Under conditions of latent labor surplus, the primary concern of employees was job security, while management was able to avail itself of cheap labor.[17]

The Postwar Family System can also be viewed as adaptive in an era of population surplus. Efficiency is not a strong point of the modern family's sexual division of labor, which assigns occupational work to men while women do full-time housework.[18] Obviously, it is far more efficient to make ability the sole criterion for placing the right person in the right job, regardless of gender. But just as Japanese-style management served to keep the latent labor surplus on company payrolls, we could also regard the sexual division of labor as having served to keep women at home, where they were categorized as housewives rather than as unemployed. Moreover, by attaching women to men, one on one, the division of labor doubtless served as an invaluable "countermeasure" to prevent unemployment and social unrest.

Conditions in Japan today, however, are very different. There is now a chronic labor shortage. Economic recession may disguise this problem in the short term, but a chronic situation will persist over the long term, due to the marked decline in population in the younger generations. The first consequence of this labor shortage has been the increased employment of women, dating from the 1980s.

It should be strongly emphasized that the labor shortage affects not only the industrial sector; the domestic labor force is also in short supply. Since the female population has been declining at the same rate as the male, even if every woman was a full-time housewife, in the area of home care of the elderly there would be a situation comparable with the industrial labor shortage. But in addition, increasing numbers of women have moved from domestic to paid labor to make up the shortfall in the corporate world. The housework "industry" may in fact be experiencing the most acute labor shortage of all. Rejecting a position that offers low status, no pay, and a demoralizing sense of being supported by their husbands, women have escaped to other industries, thus exacerbating the domestic labor shortage.

This is a more serious problem than one might imagine. As Japanese society begins to age at a very rapid rate, the care of the elderly cannot be secured by fiscal means alone. Workers will also be needed.

An individual's standard of living, I have come to think, is made up of at least three components.[19] They are money, leisure, and what economists would call "personal services." Usually people take into account only the first two, at most. But the necessity of the third component is too important to overlook. And the overwhelming majority of these necessary services are performed in the form of housework.

It is not enough to hand over a sum of money to an elderly person and say, "Here, go out and buy your favorite kind of care." There are basic minimum requirements of care which some human being has to be involved in supplying. If this work is to take the form of housework, the domestic labor shortage will have extremely serious consequences.

Readers may be familiar with the Japanese word *karoshi*, meaning death from overwork. The term usually applies to company employees, and in such cases there is now a system of compensation for deaths that are legally recognized as *karoshi*. But people also die as a result of domestic labor. It happens all the time—especially where home care is involved. One hears of many cases where, say, a woman in her sixties looking after a mother-in-law in her eighties suffers a stroke and dies first. While this situation certainly arouses sympathy, it is not certifiable as a death from overwork. But surely, since she died doing the work she was required to do, this is a case of *karoshi*. Whatever we call them, we can expect a rapid rise in the number of such cases from now on.

The corporate labor shortage has been partially filled by hiring women, but how will the domestic labor shortage be solved? We will probably see some movement toward marketization through the provision of commercial housework services; even so, it will almost certainly be impossible to manage unless men participate in housework. Society cannot cope with a labor shortage while reserving certain types of work exclusively for men or women. In future, the inefficiency of the gender-based division of labor is likely to become increasingly obvious—even, at times, cruelly obvious.

When I was teaching at a school for district nurses, I had the students analyze the district caseload with regard to the gender of the care recipient and caregiver in each case. We were interested in seeing how the division of labor by gender affected home care of the elderly, whether for better or worse, and also in looking at whether role changes occurred during the care process.

The most interesting cases from this viewpoint were those where a husband was required to look after his wife. In this situation, a certain type of couple was able to rise above the division of labor by gender. One man in the students' study had quit his company job to become a taxi driver when his wife fell ill. This meant he could be at home in the daytime one day in three, in order to do the shopping and nurse his wife. Of course, if there had been a home-care leave system for men, he would not have had to quit his job in the first place.[20]

There were other couples who took the opposite route. One husband had often consoled his sick wife, telling her, "You poor thing, you didn't deserve this. You've always done your best." But it had never crossed his mind to look after her himself—he never even attempted to do housework. And so she had dragged herself around the house to cook his meals, clean, and do the laundry. She too seems to have viewed care-giving as her job, and to have felt that her existence would lose its meaning if she received help. But then she broke a bone in a fall and ended up bedridden. This was a sorry case indeed.

It has sometimes been argued that we should rely on volunteers to care for the elderly, but the danger of this approach is that the availability of unpaid volunteers, however well-intentioned, will unfairly depress wage levels for professional home care workers. This in turn may discourage able workers from entering the field and lower its status in the eyes of the public. Behind the idea of volunteerism there seems to be a sense of guilt over placing home care on a paid basis, since it is perceived as domestic labor which should be performed free. But to define certain territory as housework, and hence the proper responsibility of the housewife, is to be blinkered by the ideal of the modern family. Here, too, the old framework has become an obstacle to problem-solving.

Chapter 10

Toward a Society with the Individual As Unit

THE ARRIVAL OF THE NEW MAN

To conclude this exploration of the formation and gradual decline of the twentieth-century family, one question remains to be asked: where is the family heading as we stand on the threshold of the twenty-first century? In sociology, it is always extremely risky to predict the future. But when society is in flux to the degree that it is today, it is no longer helpful merely to point out the need for change. Change to what? is what people want to know—and they are looking for answers that are not just *should*s or wishful thinking. Using all the available clues, how clearly can we forecast the direction that the twenty-first-century family will take?

Let us begin by looking at an example that will be familiar to many. Lately, friends of mine have been getting divorced one after another. But the fact that the divorce statistics are on the rise is no longer news in itself. What caused me to take notice was the qualitative change that these divorces represent. One couple in particular surprised everyone who knew them. These two had been in a rock band together at college, the man on vocals and the woman on keyboard. They were a strikingly well-matched couple.

This was how the husband explained the decision to end their marriage. Even after he took a corporate job, he couldn't bring himself to give up his music, and so he spent part of every paycheck on new instruments or recording studio equipment. These not only took up room in the house but eventually cut into their finances, and his wife, who as a full-time housewife was responsible for the household budget, objected to his purchases as if she had every right to complain. (In Japan, many husbands hand over their pay envelopes to their wives, who control the household finances.) After this had happened a number of times, he thought to himself: "If it means I have to give up the things I love, I've had enough of marriage. I'm not going to be reduced to a wage slave to support a wife and child who don't understand me."

To some people this might seem a shocking dereliction of a lifetime commitment which a man makes when he marries, namely, to support his wife and children. Walking out on this commitment for the sake of a hobby may seem a particular affront to male standards of decency and responsibility. But divorced men in their twenties and thirties often have similar stories to tell, and some men give similar reasons for not getting married in the first place. One man I heard of told his girlfriend, when she pressured him to marry her: "But then I couldn't go to a movie whenever I felt like it. That's not how I want to live."

While some might regard these men as hopelessly self-centered and irresponsible, I see the situation a little differently. In the eighties, women's exodus from the housewife role arose from a desire to be themselves, not domestic robots, and not the idealized wives and mothers of the "home dramas." If men are now deciding they want to be themselves and not mere bringers-home of paychecks, who can blame them?

Ever since the eighties were declared "the age of women," we have been hearing that men are not changing as fast as women. And all this time women have been issuing a challenge: where, they asked, were the new men who were not bound by gender roles and would not let the company rule their lives? But when the new men finally showed up, they were not quite what women had bargained on. For it seems to me that women in the eighties were counting on men to stay the same in one respect: to continue bringing home a paycheck. Yet the first thing that the younger generation of men apparently learned from the contemporary questioning of gender roles is that they can be liberated from the most burdensome aspect of the traditional male role, namely, having to support a wife and children. Thus, we are currently entering a new stage in the reorganization of gender roles—one which goes even further than women may have had in mind.

THE SECOND DEMOGRAPHIC TRANSITION

We will return later to the subject of changing gender roles. But first, let us take an overview of the changes that are occurring in Japanese families. When people have raised the alarm over a "crisis of the family" in Japan, they have probably had in mind the rising divorce rate and declining birthrate, together with growing numbers of unmarried couples living together and unmarried mothers. But quite apart from value judgements, how far do the facts actually support such an interpretation? Also, is there any truth in the commonly heard view that, unlike families in the West, the family in Japan is likely to survive largely unchanged? Clearly, we need to look at the statistics, and to place them in an international perspective.

Figure 10-1 shows trends in the divorce rates (per 1,000 population) of Japan and several Western countries. The rise in the Japanese rate which began in the 1970s and continued into the early 1980s was cited as evidence that the family was in crisis. A subsequent decrease brought reassurance that the Japanese family was sound after all—but not for long, as the rate began to climb again in 1989. Compared to Western nations, however, Japan has one of the lowest divorce rates. The United States, with the highest, is in a category all its own, followed by a group which includes Sweden and the United Kingdom. It should be remembered, however, that there are regional differences in divorce levels within Europe. Some European countries actually have lower divorce rates than Japan. In the strongly Catholic countries of Southern Europe, divorce remained restricted or even prohibited by law until quite recently.[1]

But divorce rates taken out of context can be a misleading indicator, because there can be no divorce without marriage. In parts of Europe, especially Scandinavia, cohabitation without legal formalities is so widespread that it could be called an alternative institution. This is not the case in the United States.

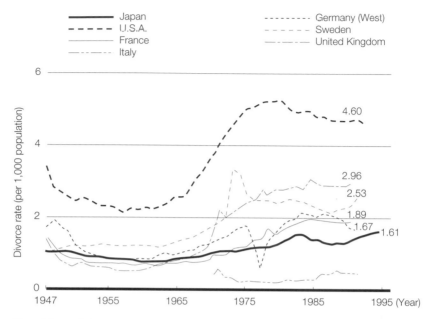

Fig. 10-1. Divorce rates in selected countries, 1947–1995

Source: Japan: Statistics and Information Department, Ministry of Health and Welfare, *Jinko dotai tokei* (Vital Statistics). Other countries: United Nations, *Demographic Yearbook*.

Americans tend to marry, divorce, and remarry; hence the exceptionally high rates of both marriage and divorce in that society.

Figure 10-2 shows marriage rates (per 1,000 population) in Japan and several Western countries. In the 1960s, cohabitation was not yet generally accepted, even in Scandinavia, but by 1972 or 1973 it had already come to be viewed as normal rather than deviant behavior.[2] Today, Europeans in their forties or younger—even people of quite solid social status—will often introduce their partner not as their wife or husband but as their girlfriend or boyfriend. These days there is nothing out of the ordinary about this, though many Japanese might think it scandalous. For although couples in Japan commonly have sexual relations before marriage, cohabitation is still far from commonplace. A couple may live together for a short period, but they tend to quickly formalize their marriage. The decline in the Japanese marriage rate is mainly due to people marrying at a later age.

Fig. 10-2. Marriage rates in selected countries, 1947–1995

Source: Japan: Statistics and Information Department, Ministry of Health and Welfare, Jinko dotai tokei (Vital Statistics). Other countries: United Nations, Demographic Yearbook.

As a natural consequence of increasing cohabitation, we also find an increase in the number of children born to nonmarried parents. Reflecting the incidence of cohabitation, Scandinavia has a high rate of extramarital births, the United States a lower one. Since about half the babies born in Sweden are born outside marriage,[3] discrimination against so-called illegitimate children is unheard of there. Lately, even in Japan there have been media reports suggesting that women are choosing to have children without marrying,[4] but by international standards this is utterly unfounded. As shown in figure 10-3, the rate of extramarital births in Japan is extremely low compared to the West: one-tenth that of Germany, one-twentieth that of the United States or Britain, and less than one-fortieth those of the Scandinavian nations. This low rate can be attributed to the existence in Japan of deep-rooted legal and social discrimination against children

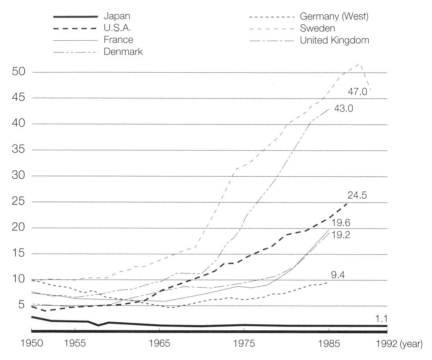

Fig. 10-3. Extramarital fertility rates in selected countries, 1950–92

Source: Japan: Statistics and Information Department, Ministry of Health and Welfare, *Jinko dotai tokei* (Vital Statistics). Other countries: United Nations, *Demographic Yearbook*.

born out of wedlock. While reform of the Civil Code to allow legitimate and illegitimate children to inherit equally is under consideration, the recent Supreme Court ruling that the existing discriminatory provisions are constitutional indicates how deeply such attitudes are entrenched.[5]

Looking next at fertility rates for the same countries (figure 10-4), in contrast to the statistics for marriage we find Japan on the leading edge of the downward trend, along with Italy and Germany. But it should be noted that in this regard also, Europe has not shown a single uniform trend. In Northern and Western Europe, the birthrate began to go down in the late 1960s after a long baby boom, and in Sweden and Denmark it dropped below the replacement level as early as the end of that decade. (The replacement level, assuming the mortality rate of a developed nation, means a total fertility rate of 2.1.) The nations of Western

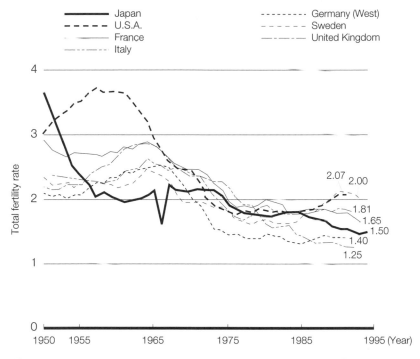

Fig. 10-4. Total fertility rates in selected countries, 1950–1994

Source: Japan: Statistics and Information Department, Ministry of Health and Welfare, *Jinko dotai tokei* (Vital Statistics). Other countries: United Nations, *Demographic Yearbook*.

Europe followed in the early seventies. Southern Europe meanwhile maintained relatively high birthrates, which seemed to suggest that, as might be expected, the Catholic countries did not fit the same pattern. Yet even in these countries, after dropping below the replacement level in the late 1970s birthrates have continued steadily downward, until Italy today has one of the world's lowest birthrates.

And where does Japan fit into this picture? Japan's birthrate could be said to show a pattern similar to Southern Europe's, both in the late start of its decline and in the rapidity of the decline once it started. In Scandinavia, by contrast, government policies providing ample support for childbirth and child rearing are proving so effective that birthrates there actually recovered to near the replacement level in the latter half of the eighties before dipping slightly again.[6]

We have now briefly surveyed a number of statistical trends, including the changing rates of divorce, cohabitation, extramarital births, and fertility, in Japan and several Western nations. Some scholars refer to such demographic changes, which began in the West at the end of the 1960s, as a second demographic transition.[7] By this they mean that these are fundamental and irreversible changes comparable in significance to the demographic transition proper (which they would call the first demographic transition), when both fertility and mortality decreased in the course of modernization. Personally, I am reluctant to apply the term "second" too lightly, lest we underemphasize the crucial importance of the original demographic transition. However, I am basically in agreement with the view that, since the 1970s, changes have been occurring in Japan and the Western nations which are transforming those societies in fundamental ways.

In the case of birthrates, I have already noted that the European regional pattern which Japan most closely resembles is that of Southern Europe, and we can perhaps identify another point that Japan has in common with this region: both still maintain a relatively conservative approach to the social norms regarding marriage.

The Japanese themselves are strongly inclined to view their society as a separate case, asserting that the family in Japan will not "break down" like those in the West. As we have just seen, however, the Western nations cannot simply be lumped together. Moreover, there is a tendency always to contrast Japan with those regions—Scandinavia, say, or the United States—where the extremes of change are seen, which makes for questionable comparisons. If we do not lose sight of the regional diversity contributed by Southern Europe, for example, it may well be possible to see the case of Japan as another regional variation of the "second demographic transition."

THE END OF THE ERA OF THE FAMILY

Where is this transition taking families in the Western nations and Japan? A very useful framework for thinking about such long-term changes in the family is provided by Michael Anderson's short article, "What Is New about the Modern Family: An Historical Perspective."[8]

The divorce statistics we looked at earlier in this chapter take on a somewhat different profile when we place them, as Anderson does, in the context of long-term family change. Anderson calculated the percentages (actual and predicted) of marriages already ended in either death or divorce after a certain number of years for marriage cohorts in England and Wales. For example, the marriages of about 30 percent of the couples in the 1980 marriage cohort (i.e., those who married in 1980) will have ended in twenty years, due either to the death of one of the spouses or to divorce. Since the gradient is essentially unchanged when the same curve is plotted for divorce alone, clearly divorce accounts for the ending of most of these marriages. In contrast, only about half as many marriages ended in the cohorts who married in 1921 and 1946. It is therefore tempting to conclude that the more recent a marriage is, the less likely it is to last. But before we jump to this conclusion, we should look at the cohorts for 1826 and 1896. Almost as many of these marriages lasted for as brief a time as those of the 1980 cohort, but for a different reason—the death of one of the partners (figure 10-5).

It may seem surprising to find that marriages in Britain were almost as short-lived in the nineteenth century as they are today, albeit for different reasons. Yet when we examine the past history of divorce in Japan, we are in for even more of a shock. For unlike European societies, where the influence of the Christian church's prohibition of divorce was strong, in Japan many more marriages ended in breakdown. Figure 10-6 shows long-term trends in Japan's divorce rate since modern statistics began to be kept. As can be seen, the rate was once so high, in fact, that until the early decades of this century Japan was known as the world's leading nation for divorce.[9] But how easily broken were Japanese marriages in the period before modernization began? In figure 10-5, I have tried plotting data for Japan in the latter half of the Tokugawa Period (1603–1867) using the same principle as Anderson's graph. The figures were calculated from the popula-

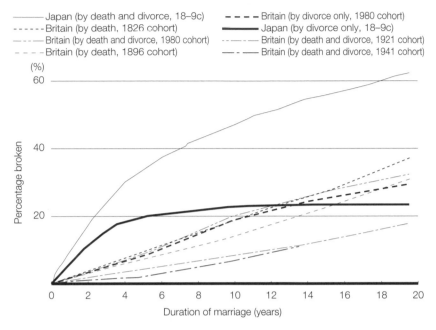

Fig. 10-5. Percentage of marriages broken, Britain and Japan

Note: "Britain" refers to England and Wales. "Japan" refers to two villages, Shimomoriya and Niita, in the
northeast region.
Source: Britain: Anderson, "What Is New about the Modern Family: An Historical Perspective."[8]
Japan: Ochiai, "Ushinawareta kazoku o motomete: Tokugawa shakai no rekishi-jinkogaku."[10]

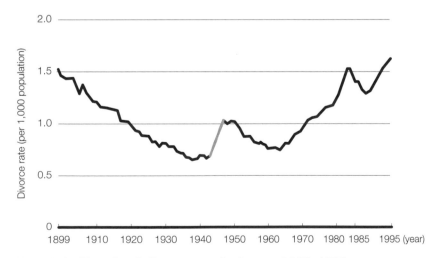

Fig. 10-6. Trends of divorce rate in Japan, 1899–1989

Sources: To 1943: Cabinet Bureau of Statistics, *Nihon teikoku tokei nenkan dai 38 kai* (Statistical yearbook of
Imperial Japan no. 38); *Nihon teikoku jinko dotai tokei* (Vital Statistics of Imperial Japan). From 1947:
Statistics and Information Department, Ministry of Health and Welfare, *Jinko dotai tokei* (Vital Statistics).

tion registers (*Ninbetsu Aratame Cho*) of two villages in the former Nihonmatsu domain, in what is now Fukushima Prefecture.[10] It turns out that almost 60 percent of the marriages in these villages ended within twenty years. A particularly large number —almost 20 percent of all marriages—ended in separation within the first five years. Thus, we find that the relative durability of contemporary Japanese marriages, far from being rooted in tradition, was newly acquired in the course of modernization, to an even greater degree than was seen in Britain.[11]

Given this context, rather than being surprised at the short-lived nature of marriages in the nineteenth century and again in our own times, we may begin to find it more remarkable that they were so stable during the intervening period. As Anderson has pointed out, the effect of the decline in mortality on family life cannot be overemphasized.[12] In moving from an uncertain world in which, even after reaching adulthood, a person might die at any time, to one where death almost always comes in old age, marriage and family life took on a permanence and stability they had never had before.

For the first time in human history, marriage and family became institutions within which one could confidently expect to live out one's life. As a corollary, life took on a greater degree of predictability and standardization; in other words, people's lives all came to resemble one another.[13] The resulting era, in which everyone pursued a similar life course and created similar families, was what we have called in previous chapters the era of the modern family. Economic factors also acted to further stabilize and standardize the family; these included the realization of full employment and the high levels of consumption in every social class which became possible in the twentieth century, particularly in the developed nations after the Second World War, in what came to be called the affluent society. And of course, as we have already seen, a major role was played by the ideology which exalted love for family and children. The modern era, particularly the twentieth century, has indeed been the era of the family.

As the twentieth century nears its end, what new era is being ushered in by the demographic changes we have been discussing?

Dirk J. van de Kaa, a leading proponent of the "second demographic transition," has summarized the trends common throughout Europe in such terms as "a shift from the golden age of marriage to the dawn of cohabitation," "a shift from the era of the king-child with parents to that of the king-pair with a child," and "a shift from uniform to pluralistic families and households."[14] Van de Kaa states clearly that the era of the modern or standardized family is at an end. To another theorist of the "second demographic transition," R. Lesthaeghe, the ongoing changes signify the arrival of full-fledged individualism, largely due to secularization, or the relaxation of religious norms, and rising consumption levels.[15] Thus we find this scenario of change emerging: the end of the era of the family, and the arrival of the individual.

A SOCIETY WHICH HAS THE INDIVIDUAL AS ITS UNIT

Among Japanese scholars also, in the last decade the term "individualization" has joined "diversification" as a signpost of the new direction of family change. The changes we noted earlier in relation to the "second demographic transition" indicate the coming of a society in which family membership is not assumed to be a necessary condition of every person's life. These changes represent the loss of the public meaning assigned to marriage, and the increasing prevalence of life courses in which one may have no spouse or children for all or a considerable part of one's lifetime. While the younger generations are actively choosing this way of life, it may also be dictated by circumstances, of course, as in the case of an elderly person who has outlived his or her spouse.

The family sociologist Meguro Yoriko was the first in Japan to clearly formulate the concept of the individualized family. Meguro sums up the concept as follows: "What this means is that family life has increasingly taken on the character of something created at a particular time by people with particular personal ties, rather than an experience taken for granted as part of life. The process whereby the individual has emerged from within the group to become a unit of social life in his or her own right can be seen as a process of change in the family. Family life thus becomes just one of a number of lifestyle options for the individual."[16]

On hearing that the age of the individual is about to dawn, Japanese readers may think, "What, again?" For after Japan's defeat in the war, when the *ie* system was originally said to have ended, the age of the "democratic family" which respected the individual was widely heralded under the influence of the United States. But what is meant this time is quite different. Where once the dawn of the new age was a slogan, urging respect for the individual as a desirable ideal, now it is a matter of observable fact that, whether we like it or not, the basic unit of the social system is already changing to the individual.[17] In the absence of any other social unit to which everyone belongs, the individual becomes the only possible basic unit of society. Writing in the 1970s, Philippe Ariès dissented from the view that modern times were the era of individualism, declaring that "it was not individualism which triumphed, but the family."[18] But now that the triumph of the family of which Ariès spoke is over, the true era of the individual may be about to begin at last.

In case there is any misunderstanding, let me add that the transition to the individual as the basic unit of society does not necessarily mean that more people will live alone. Since stable personal relationships often provide deep emotional experiences, there is every reason to think that people who are economically and practically quite capable of living on their own will nevertheless choose to live together. But the resulting "families" will differ from those of a society where the family is automatically assumed to be the basic unit, because the individuals concerned will have formed them voluntarily. And just as those who have not bought CD players are currently treated no differently from those who have, people who have not formed families will no longer be treated differently in every arena of society from those who have.

As a result, Meguro predicts, the family will change from a limiting factor for whose sake personal dreams and fulfillment must be sacrificed, to "a factor supporting the way of life chosen by the individual."[19] While we need not expect living for the sake of others to disappear entirely, it seems likely, at least, that long years of self-sacrifice for the family will no longer be demanded, or admired, as a way of life.

A recently published book by Ida Hiroyuki, *Seisabetsu to shihonsei: Shinguru tan'i shakai no teisho* (Sexism and capitalism: A proposal for a society with the single person as unit), directly addresses what I have been calling "the society with the individual as unit." Ida distinguishes clearly between the society we have known until now, which he calls the "couple-unit" or "family-unit" society, and its antithesis, the society with the single person as unit. A family-unit society is one in which it is "not the individual but the family (the husband and wife, usually with children) which is the basic unit of society, everyday living, and the economy." It is also "a society in which factors such as gender and marital status are extremely important in determining how the individual is perceived." In the society of single-person units advocated by Ida, on the other hand, the individual constitutes the basic unit of society, everyday living, and the economy, and "gender, marital status, and so on become irrelevant in determining how a person is perceived."[20]

In the family-unit society, the man is taken to represent the unit and the wife becomes "shadowed" as his dependent. Moreover, any conflict is hidden since, in principle, conflicts and oppression do not exist within these units. Thus the very existence of the family as unit is a hidden source of sexism.[21]

It is not hard to see that the Japanese society we have known in the postwar period has the family as its basic unit.[22] The employment, taxation, and pension systems, as well as the arrangements of day-to-day life, were all put together on the assumption that everyone belonged to a similar "standard family" containing a dependent married woman and two children. For instance, take the long working hours which are made possible only because there is a housewife at home; the day-care centers which will not admit children if there are family members who can look after them; the tax deductions for spouses and dependents, and the pension systems which pay out to housewives, even though neither they nor their husbands have contributed a single yen in premiums toward the housewife's pension, by imposing unfair burdens on single persons and double-income households. A wife whose earnings are below what is known as the "one million yen barrier" (currently about US$10,000) is exempted from paying income tax and social insurance premiums (in the latter case, the cutoff point is 1.3 million yen). While these appear on the surface to be natural and benign systems supporting daily life, they have served, in effect, to penalize and bring into line those who deviated from the standard. But times have changed, and those who deviate from the standard are on the way to becoming the majority. The ratio of single persons aged between 30 and 35 has exceeded 30 percent for men and 10 percent for women, and 70 percent of mothers in their forties now work outside the home. A society that continues to penalize so many of its members will not survive long.

Ida has proposed concrete reforms leading toward a society based on the single-person unit. The proposal which I think best expresses the spirit of that society concerns the handling of the issue of home care for the sick and elderly.

The question of whether to pay an allowance to family caregivers from public funds is a controversial one in contemporary Japan. Ida is against the payment of a care-giver allowance. He argues that public subsidies should be paid not to the care-giving family but to the person who requires home care. He offers the example of the Danish system whereby severely disabled persons employ their own personal helpers, receiving for this purpose a monthly public subsidy equivalent to 300,000 yen (US$3,000) per helper. This is a startling idea to anyone accustomed to think of home-care recipients as weak, helpless people supported by the love and devotion of their families, but Ida argues persuasively that "the approach based on the single-person unit means that welfare services and benefits are basically supplied directly to the elderly person, disabled adult, or child, while respecting his or her autonomy and establishing him or her as the agent who selects, purchases and uses the services, hires the helpers, and issues the requests and instructions."[23]

Contrary to the impression of warmth that it gives at first sight, home care which relies on the love and goodwill of family members or volunteers tends to force the recipient further into a position of dependency and indebtedness. This may account for the fact that Japan has one of the world's highest suicide rates for elderly women (second only to that of Hungary), and moreover that the rate is higher for women co-residing with their children than for women living alone.[24] Ida has raised some thought-provoking questions by pointing out that while liberation of the individual from the family may seem to be important primarily to those in a strong position, in fact it is an even more urgent concern for the weak.

THE PROBLEM OF THE HOUSEWIFE

Japan's civil law is currently undergoing the most extensive review process since the new Civil Code was drawn up after the Second World War. When one lists the points contained in the reform proposals, many of them appear to lead toward a society with the individual as its basic unit. For example, there is the proposal to allow married couples the option of retaining separate surnames (but with their children all taking the same name); the proposal to introduce a new system in which a divorce is granted after five years' separation, even when sought by the party at fault; and the elimination of discrimination against illegitimate children in the inheritance law. The principles that can be seen to underlie these proposed reforms are that individuals' lives should not have to change depending on whether or not they belong to a family, and that families will no longer be specially protected to ensure the maintenance of the status quo.

These reforms are sometimes said to benefit women, but the situation is not so straightforward. To be sure, more women than men support the proposal for separate surnames, but when it comes to recognizing divorce after five years' separation, strong opposition and concern has been voiced by women who see this as allowing husbands to get away with unfaithfulness. Further, with regard to removing discrimination against illegitimate children, married women seeking to protect the interests of their children are in a position diametrically opposed to that of women who have had children outside marriage. These days, there is no single position that could be defined as "the woman's viewpoint." To put it plainly, women's attitudes toward individualization are split down the middle according to whether or not they want to protect the status of wives.

The arrival of the individualized society seems certain to have the greatest impact on the housewife. Feminists in the eighties often declared that men who could not even look after themselves were no more independent than housewives. But one is forced to admit that this argument does not really stand up, except as sarcasm, because the fact is that a man whose wife has left him can "individualize" while living on boxed lunches and the like bought from a convenience store, but a housewife whose husband stops bringing home his pay is left high and dry.

Faced with this impact, the housewife probably does not have the option of continuing as she is now. It seems to me that three conditions are necessary for a housewife to be secure: her husband does not die, he does not lose his job, and they do not divorce. The first condition is firmly in place, thanks to the demographic transition; but with full employment crumbling and the divorce rate on the rise, the second and third are increasingly fragile. To choose to become a housewife under these circumstances takes either a good deal of courage or an extremely optimistic outlook. It has been suggested that the recession which followed the collapse of Japan's economic bubble has brought an end to women's exodus from the housewife role, but this is clearly nonsense. Who could stay at home with any sense of security when the recession means her husband may lose his job at any time? The rise of female employment rates in Europe and the United States since the 1970s was partly a reflection of the harsh reality that, in a time of chronic economic slowdown, women had lost the security of being able to depend on a man's income for life. Today independence is no longer simply a question of ideals.

The institutional reforms now under way encompass not only revision of the Civil Code but also review of the pension and social security systems, strengthening of the Equal Employment Opportunity Law, and a bill to provide home care insurance.

What makes me very uneasy about the moves in this direction is the fact that there has been little, if any, discussion of how the various reforms are interrelated, even though a major focus of debate in each case is the social position of women, and particularly of housewives. (The fact that each is the responsibility of a separate ministry may be partly to blame.) Thus, while revision of the Civil Code will make divorce easier, a proposal to institute penalties under the Equal Employment Opportunity Law has again been shelved, and blatant discrimination against female job applicants was rampant during the post-bubble recession. Under these conditions, how are women expected to live when their "permanent job" (a jesting expression for a woman's marriage) is no longer permanent, and yet they are barred from corporate jobs? The Ministry of International Trade and Industry wants to use women as corporate labor, the Ministry of Health and Welfare is counting on them to provide home care. Since women are only human, how they can be expected to fulfill all these opportunistic demands is beyond me.

Policymakers should acknowledge that the current reforms are heading, as a whole, toward a soft landing in a society whose unit is the individual, and that during the transition the greatest problem will undoubtedly be the treatment of the social group of housewives, a group who, although they are adults, cannot become individuals as a social unit. Policymakers need to acknowledge this both to make sure that they know what they are doing, and to obtain informed consent to their social remedies. Perhaps they are saying nothing to avoid hurting housewives' feelings, but their considerateness will have the reverse effect. At this rate, before we know it women may fall through the cracks of institutional reform and find themselves in a no-win situation, where neither becoming a housewife nor choosing another way of life is a workable option. We must have more discussion, and we must reform the system in such a way that women's lives in the future can be clearly envisioned. For Japanese women, this is the critical moment.

Notes

Prologue: The Twentieth-Century Family As Starting Point

1. Ochiai Emiko, "Decent Housewives and Sensual White Women: Representations of Women of Postwar Japanese Magazines," *Japan Review* (International Research Center for Japanese Studies) 9 (1997): 151–169; Ochiai Emiko, "Bijuaru imeji toshite no onna" (Women as visual image), in Joseishi Sogo Kenkyukai, ed., *Nihon josei seikatsushi* (A history of the daily lives of Japanese women), vol. 5: *Gendai* (The present) (Tokyo: University of Tokyo Press, 1990), 203–34.

2. The poor ratings of the NHK television drama *Kimi no na wa* (What's your name?) can probably be seen as evidence of this. The drama was a 1991 remake of an immensely popular radio series (1952–54) and three-part movie (1953–54), taking its theme from the earliest days after the war.

1. Have Women Always Been Housewives?

1. Takahashi Hisako, ed., *Kawariyuku fujin rodo* (Women's labor in transition) (Tokyo: Yuhikaku, 1983), 2–6. The female labor force participation rates I have cited here are slightly different from those shown for Japan in Figure 1-3; this is because the cited figures are from the *Rodoryoku chosa* (Labor force survey), while those in Figure 1-3 are from the National Census.

2. Mizuno Asao, ed., *Keizai sofutoka jidai no josei rodo* (Female labor in the age of the soft economy) (Tokyo: Yuhikaku, 1984), 4. Mizuno relied on the following sources to prepare the figure:
   United States: *The Historical Statistics of the United States from Colonial Times to the Present* (Washington, D.C.: Census Bureau), 133; *Employment and Training Report of the President* (Washington, D.C., 1982), 150, 212.
   United Kingdom: G. Joseph, *Women at Work* (Oxford: Allan Philip, 1983), 126–7; *Employment Gazette* 91, no. 2 (February 1983): 51.
   France: Okada Minoru, "Furansu keizai katsudo jinko no kozo to hatten" (Structure and development of the economically active population of France), in Chuo University Institute of Economic Research, ed., *Keizai seicho to shugyo kozo* (Economic growth and employment structures) (Tokyo: Toyo Keizai Shinposha, 1973), 192; A.M. Yohalem, ed., *Women Returning to Work: Policies and Progress in Five Countries* (London: Frances Pinter, 1980), 63.
   West Germany: W. Müller, A. Willms, and J. Handl, *Strukturwandel der Frauenarbeit 1880-1980* (Frankfurt: Campus Verlag, 1983), 35; Statistisches Bundesamt, *Statistisches Jahrbuch* (Bonn, 1981), 94.
   Sweden: Yohalem, op. cit., 112.
   Japan: Prime Minister's Office, Statistics Bureau, *Jinko no shugyo jotai to sangyo kosei* (The employment situation and industrial composition of the population), 1980 Census Monograph Series, no. 4 (Tokyo, 1983), 37.

3. Anita Nyberg, "The Social Construction of Married Women's Labour-Force Participation: The Case of Sweden in the Twentieth Century," *Continuity and Change* 9, no. 1 (1994): 145–156.

4. In the fields of family history and women's history, there has been a consensus in recent years that modernization was not a unidirectional process of liberation for women (or children).

5. Sechiyama has studied differences in the housewifization process due to differences in ethnicity and social systems in four regions: China, Taiwan, North Korea, and South Korea. Sechiyama Kaku, *Higashi-Ajia no kafuchosei* (East Asian patriarchal systems) (Tokyo: Keiso Shobo, 1996).

2. The Origins of Housework and the Housewife

1. Ann Oakley, *Housewife* (London: Allen Lane, 1974); published in the U.S. as *Woman's Work: The Housewife, Past and Present* (New York: Pantheon, 1974). The first definition is quoted from Audrey Hunt, *A Survey of Women's Employment* (London: Government Social Survey, HMSO, 1968). The second is from the Oxford English Dictionary.

2. Ishigaki Ayako, "Shufu to iu daini shokugyo ron" (The secondary occupation of homemaking), *Fujin koron*, February 1955, reprinted in Ueno Chizuko, ed., *Shufu ronso o yomu I* (Reading the housewife debate, part 1) (Tokyo: Keiso Shobo, 1982).

3. Shimizu Keiko, "Shufu no jidai wa hajimatta" (The age of the housewife has begun), *Fujin koron*, April 1955, reprinted in Ueno, *Shufu ronso* (see note 2).

4. Umesao Tadao, "Tsuma muyo ron" (The superfluous wife), *Fujin koron*, June 1959, reprinted in Ueno, *Shufu ronso* (see note 2).

5. For the domestic labor debate in Britain, see Susan Himmelweit and Simon Mohun, "Domestic Labour and Capital," *Cambridge Journal of Economics* 1, no. 1 (1977); Takenaka Emiko, "Rodoryoku saiseisan no shihonshugiteki seikaku to kaji rodo: Kaji rodo o meguru saikin no ronso ni yosete" (Domestic labor and the capitalistic nature of the reproduction of labor power: A contribution to the recent debate on domestic labor), *Keizaigaku zasshi* (Osaka City University) 81, no. 1 (1980); and Kuba Yoshiko, "Kaji rodo to seikatsu yoshiki: Himmelweit-Mohan 'Kaji rodo to shihon' o yonde" (Domestic labor and lifestyle: A reading of Himmelweit and Mohan's "Domestic Labour and Capital"), *Keizai hyoron*, March 1979.

6. Christine Delphy, *Close to Home: A Materialist Analysis of Women's Oppression*, trans. Diana Leonard (Amherst: University of Massachusetts Press, 1984), 16.

7. Kawagoe Osamu, Himeoka Toshiko, Harada Hitomi, and Wakahara Norikazu, *Kindai o ikiru onnatachi* (Women's lives in the modern age) (Tokyo: Miraisha, 1990).

8. Himeoka Toshiko, *Kindai Doitsu no boseishugi feminizumu* (Maternalist feminism in modern Germany) (Tokyo: Keiso Shobo, 1993).

9. Tsunoyama Sakae, "Katei to shohi seikatsu" (The home and consumer life), in Tsunoyama Sakae and Kawakita Minoru, ed., *Rojiura no Daiei Teikoku* (The British Empire in back alleys) (Tokyo: Heibonsha, 1982). Various abridged and revised editions of Mrs. Beeton's cookbook are still in print today.

10. Yvonne Verdier, *Façons de dire, façons de faire* (Paris: Gallimard, 1979), Chapter 3.

11. Nishikawa Yuko, "Sumai no hensen to 'katei' no seiritsu" (Changes in housing and the formation of "the home"), in Joseishi Sogo Kenkyukai, ed., *Nihon josei seikatsushi* (A history of the daily lives of Japanese women), vol. 4: *Kindai* (The modern era) (Tokyo: University of Tokyo Press, 1990).

12. Chimoto Akiko, "Nihon ni okeru seibetsu yakuwari bungyo no keisei: Kakei chosa o toshite" (The formation of the sexual division of roles in Japan, as seen in household budget surveys), in Ogino Miho, Chimoto Akiko, Ochiai Emiko et al., *Seido toshite no 'onna'* ("Woman" as institution) (Tokyo: Heibonsha, 1990), 187–228.

13. Economic Planning Agency, *Kokumin seikatsu hakusho Showa 35 nendoban* (White paper on the national life for fiscal 1960) (Tokyo, 1960).

3. The Two-Child Revolution

1. Ato Makoto, "Wagakuni saikin no shusseiritsu teika no bunseki" (An analysis of the recent decline of the Japanese birthrate), *Jinkogaku kenkyu* 5 (1982): 17–24.

2. In Japan, and in other East Asian countries such as China and South Korea, reliance on abortion has remained relatively high even after scientific methods of contraception such as surgical sterilization and the Pill became available. The practice may be deeply rooted in cultural traditions whose underlying concepts of life and death include, among other elements, the view that the fetus is not a human being, and the Buddhist belief in reincarnation. For a discussion of the conflicts between modernization and such cultural traditions, see Ochiai Emiko, "Kinseimatsu ni okeru mabiki to shussan" (Infanticide and childbirth at the end of the early modern period), in Wakita Haruko and Susan Hanley, eds., *Jenda no Nihonshi* (The history of gender in Japan), vol. 1, (Tokyo: University of Tokyo Press, 1994), 425–459; Ochiai Emiko, "The Reproductive Revolution at the End of the Tokugawa Period," in Tonomura Hitomi, Ann Walthall and Wakita Haruko, eds., *Women and Class in Japanese History* (Ann Arbor: University of Michigan Press, forthcoming).

3. Muramatsu Minoru, "Abortion in Modern Japan," presented to the IUSSP-IRCJS Workshop on "Abortion, Infanticide and Neglect in Asian History," held at the International Research Center for Japanese Studies, Kyoto, 1994.

4. I would like to thank Ms. Yoshimura Noriko for allowing me to accompany her during her research. According to her findings, it is not unusual for women to have undergone ten or more surgical abortions. See Yoshimura Noriko, *Kodomo o umu* (To bear a child) (Tokyo: Iwanami Shoten, 1992), 142.

5. Gary S. Becker, "An Economic Analysis of Fertility," in National Bureau of Economic Research, *Demographic and Economic Change in Developed Countries* (Princeton: Princeton University Press, 1960); Gary S. Becker, *A Treatise on the Family* (Cambridge, Mass.: Harvard University Press, 1981).

6. The completed number of children per couple can only be calculated for those cohorts that have completed their reproductive years.

7. Philippe Ariès, *L'enfant et la vie familiale sous l'ancien régime* (Paris: Seuil, 1960). Ariès's method has been subject to various criticisms and his findings cannot be accepted without question, but nevertheless, there is no denying his great contributions in pioneering the study of *mentalité* with regard to children, and in raising the issue of the evolution of the modern concept of childhood.

8. Ibid., 77.

9. Elisabeth Badinter, *L'amour en plus* (Paris: Flammarion, 1980). Published in English as *The Myth of Motherhood* (London: Souvenir Press, 1981) and *Mother Love: Myth and Reality* (New York: Macmillan, 1981).

10. Linda Pollock, *Forgotten Children* (Cambridge: Cambridge University Press, 1983).

11. Françoise Loux, *Le jeune enfant et son corps dans la médicine traditionelle* (Paris: Flammarion, 1978).

12. Honoré de Balzac, *The Marriage Contract* (Boston: Roberts Brothers, 1894; London: J. M. Dent, 1879), 42, quoted in Badinter, *Mother Love: Myth and Reality*, 186.

13. Kyutoku Shigemori, *Bogenbyo* (Maternally induced diseases) (Tokyo: Kyoiku Kenkyusha, 1979; reprint, Tokyo: Sanmaku Shuppan, 1991).

14. Ibid., 23–24.

15. Ibid., 24.

16. Jacques Donzelot, *La police des familles* (Paris: Editions de Minuit, 1977), Chapter 2.

17. John Hajnal, "European Marriage Pattern in Perspective," in D. V. Glass and D. E. C. Eversley, eds., *Population in History* (London: Edward Arnold, 1965).

18. Ansley J. Coale, "The Decline of Fertility in Europe from the French Revolution to World War II," in S. J. Behrman et al., eds., *Fertility and Family Planning* (Ann Arbor: University of Michigan Press, 1969); Ansley J. Coale and Susan Cotts Watkins, eds., *The Decline of Fertility in Europe* (Princeton: Princeton University Press, 1986).

4. **The Truth about the Nuclearization of the Family**
1. George P. Murdock, *Social Structure* (New York: Macmillan, 1949), Chapter 1.
2. Yuzawa Yasuhiko, *Zusetsu gendai Nihon no kazoku mondai* (An illustrated study of family issues in modern Japan) (Tokyo: Japan Broadcast Publishing, 1987), 6–7.
3. Ito Tatsuya, "Dojidai o keisei suru hitobito" (The people who form an era), *Kyoiku to joho* (Ministry of Education), no. 380 (1989), reprinted in Ito, *Seikatsu no naka no jinkogaku* (Demography in everyday life) (Tokyo: Kokin Shoin, 1994), 187–212.
4. For a discussion of images of the family in postwar Japanese TV dramas, see Ochiai Emiko, "Terebi no kazokutachi wa doshite kagayaku no ka" (Why are television's families radiant?), in *Bessatsu takarajima 110: 80-nendai no shotai* (Takarajima special issue 110: The true nature of the 80s) (Tokyo: JICC, 1990).
5. Ito Tatsuya, "*Seikatsu no naka no jinkogaku*" (see note 3), 190–191.
6. Ibid., 194.
7. Hiroshima Kiyoshi, *Sengo Nihon ni okeru oya to ko no dokyoritsu no jinkogakuteki jissho bunseki* (A demographic analysis of the ratio of parent-child co-residence in postwar Japan), *Jinko mondai kenkyu* (Institute of Population Problems, Ministry of Health and Welfare) 169 (1984): 31–42; Hiroshima Kiyoshi, "Recent Change in Prevalence of Parent-Child Co-residence in Japan," *Jinkogaku kenkyu* (Population Association of Japan) 10: 31–40.
8. William H. Whyte, *The Organization Man* (New York: Simon and Schuster, 1956), 351.
9. Masuda Kokichi, "Tekkin apato kyoju kazoku no neighboring" (Neighbor interaction among resident families in ferro-concrete apartment buildings), *Konan daigaku bungakkai ronshu* 11 (1960).
10. Koyama Takashi, "Nihon ni okeru shinzoku kankei no noson to toshi no hikaku" (A comparison of kin relations in rural and urban Japan), in *Daikyukai kokusai kazoku kenkyu semina hokokusho* (Report of the 9th International Family Research Seminar) (Tokyo: Japan National Committee for UNESCO, 1966), 47.
11. Morioka Kiyomi, Honma Jun, Yamaguchi Tazuko, and Takao Atsuko, "Tokyo kinko danchi kazoku no seikatsushi to shakai sanka" (A history of daily life and social participation of families in suburban Tokyo housing complexes), *Kokusai Kirisutokyo Daigaku gakuho IIB: Shakai kagaku janaru* 7 (1968): 263.
12. Masuda, "Tekkin apato," 11 (see note 9).
13. For a detailed comparison of the social networks of families in the 1960s and the 1980s, see Ochiai Emiko, "Kazoku no shakaiteki nettowaku to jinkogakuteki sedai: 60-nendai to 80-nendai no hikaku kara" (The social networks of families and the demographic generations: From a comparison of the 1960s and the 1980s), in Hasumi Otohiko and Okuda Michio, ed., *Nijuisseiki Nihon no neo-komyunite* (Neo-communities in twenty-first-century Japan) (Tokyo: University of Tokyo Press, 1993), 101–130.

5. **The Postwar Family System**
1. Ochiai Emiko, *Kindai kazoku to feminizumu* (The modern family and feminism) (Tokyo: Keiso Shobo, 1989).
2. Kawashima Takeyoshi, *Nihon shakai no kazokuteki kosei* (The familial structure of Japanese society) (Tokyo: Gakusei Shobo, 1948), 3.
3. Ochiai Emiko, "Kindai kazoku no tanjo to shuen" (The birth and death of the modern family), *Gendai shiso* 13, no. 6 (1985), reprinted in Ochiai, *Kindai kazoku to feminizumu*, 2–24 (see note 1).
4. Alvin Gouldner, *The Coming Crisis of Western Sociology* (New York: Basic Books, 1970), Chapter 2.
5. Willard Waller, *The Family: A Dynamic Interpretation* (New York: Holt, Rinehart and Winston, 1938), revised version by Reuben Hill published from the same publisher in 1951; Norman W. Bell and Ezra F. Vogel, *A Modern Introduction to the Family* (New

York: Free Press, 1960); Morioka Kiyomi and Mochizuki Takashi, *Atarashii Kazoku Shakaigaku* (New family sociology) (Tokyo: Baifukan, 1983). For further discussion, see Ochiai Emiko, "Kazoku shakaigaku no paradaimu tenkan" (The paradigm shift in family sociology), Chapter 6 in Ochiai, *Kindai kazoku to feminizumu*, 136–69 (see note 1).

6. Talcott Parsons and Robert F. Bales, *Family: Socialization and Interaction Process* (London: Routledge & Kegan Paul, 1956).

7. Such a framework is also clearly discernible in the prewar writings of the pioneering Japanese sociologist Toda Teizo. See Toda Teizo, *Kazoku kosei* (Family composition) (Tokyo: Kobundo, 1937). Broadly speaking, it may have been Japan's position in the modern world which made a framework of this kind necessary, rather than the experience of defeat in the war per se.

8. Kazoku Mondai Kenkyukai, ed., *Yamamuro Shuhei chosakushu: Kazoku gakusetsushi no kenkyu* (Collected writings of Yamamuro Shuhei: An historical study of family theory) (Tokyo: Kakiuchi Shuppan, 1987), 308.

6. Women's Liberation and the Dissolution of the Family

1. Ehara Yumiko's "Karakai no seijigaku" (The politics of ridicule) is an accurate analysis of power relations in the contemporary media coverage of women's lib. In Ehara Yumiko, *Josei kaiho to iu shiso* (The ideology of women's liberation) (Tokyo: Keiso Shobo, 1985), 172–94.

2. Tanaka Mitsu for the Josei Kaiho Renraku Kaigi Junbikai, "Benjo kara no kaiho" (Liberation from being toilets), August 1970, reprinted in Mizoguchi Akiyo, Saeki Yoko, and Miki Soko, eds., *Shiryo Nihon uman ribu shi* (History of Japanese women's lib in documents), vol. 1 (Kyoto: Shokado, 1992), 205.

3. Mizoguchi Akiyo, Saeki Yoko, and Miki Soko, eds., *Shiryo Nihon uman ribu shi* (History of Japanese women's lib in documents), 3 vols. (Kyoto: Shokado, 1992–95). (Volume 1 is hereafter cited as Hist. JWL.)

4. Metoroparichen, October 21, 1970, reprinted in Hist. JWL, 148.

5. Josei Kaiho Renraku Kaigi Junbikai, August 1970, reprinted in Hist. JWL, 201. *Gebaruto Roza*, from the German *Gewalt* (force) and the name Rosa (Luxemburg), was the nickname of a Japanese student radical famed for her courage.

6. Mori Setsuko for Shiso Shudan S-E-X, May 14, 1970, reprinted in Hist. JWL, 172.

7. The series entitled "Onna no ronri" (Woman's logic) by Kono Nobuko, which appeared in the local journal *Mumei tsushin*, is particularly well known. Portions of this series were later published in book form under the same title (Fukuoka: Ryukasonjuku Shuppan, 1973).

8. Mori Setsuko for Shiso Shudan S-E-X, May 14, 1970, reprinted in Hist. JWL, 175.

9. Ibid., 172.

10. Nakayama Kiyoko for *Les femmes*, "Otokotachi e" (To men), July 4, 1971, reprinted in Hist. JWL, 71.

11. Group Kunoichi, October 30, 1971, reprinted in Hist. JWL, 137.

12. Ibid., 127.

13. Tanaka Mitsu for the Josei Kaiho Renraku Kaigi Junbikai, "Benjo kara no kaiho" (Liberation from being toilets), August 1970, reprinted in Hist. JWL, 206.

14. Ibid., 205.

15. The two most widely known women's lib groups were Shinjuku Lib Center, which carried on the work of Group Tatakau Onna (Fighting Women), and Chupiren (Chuzetsukinshiho ni Hantai Shi Piru Kaikin o Yokyu Suru Joseikaiho Rengo, or the Women's Liberation Alliance to Oppose the Anti-Abortion Law and Demand Repeal of the Ban on the Pill), who were spotlighted as representatives of women's lib due to their pink helmets and the media appeal of their tactics. The groups' policy differences are well illustrated by two typical slogans: Fighting Women's "Toward a society worthy of giving birth," and Chupiren's "Woman's right to choose."

For further discussion (in Japanese) of the different groups that made up the women's lib movement in Japan, see: Inoue Teruko, *Joseigaku to sono shuhen* (Women's studies and related areas) (Tokyo: Keiso Shobo, 1980); Ehara, *Josei kaiho to iu shiso* (see note 1); Fujieda Mioko, "Uman ribu" (Women's lib), in *Onna no sengoshi* (Women's postwar history) (Tokyo: Asahi Shimbunsha, 1985); Akiyama Yoko, "Enoki Misako to Chupiren: Ribu shishi noto" (Enoki Misako and the Chupiren: Notes toward a personal history of women's lib), in *Joseigaku nenpo* 12 (1991): 109–115, for a critique of the Chupiren from the viewpoint of a participant in the contemporary movement; Ueno Terumasa, "Shussan o meguru ishiki henka to josei no kenri" (Women's rights and changing attitudes regarding childbirth) in Joseishi Sogo Kenkyukai, ed., *Nihon josei seikatsushi* (A history of the daily lives of Japanese women), vol. 5: *Gendai* (The present) (Tokyo: University of Tokyo Press, 1990), 101–131. As an introduction to the women's movement, the last-mentioned essay overemphasizes the Chupiren, but it is useful for a detailed account of the attempt to revise the Eugenic Protection Law.

For a general discussion of the women's lib movement in Japan, see: Inoue Haneko et al., *Asatte ni niji o kakeru* (Stretching a rainbow to the day after tomorrow) (Kyoto: Tokarajisha, 1986); "Tokushu: Ribu nijusshunen" (Special feature: 20th anniversary of women's lib), *Inpakushon* 73 (February 1992); "Tokushu: Feminizumu jusoteki shihai kozo o utsu" (Special feature: Feminism critiques the multilayered power structure), *Jokyo*, June 1992.

16. Group Tatakau Onna, December 1970, reprinted in Hist. JWL, 224.

17. Hist. JWL, 162.

18. Sasaki Kazuko for Group Tatakau Onna, October 1970, reprinted in Hist. JWL, 212.

19. Tanaka Mitsu for Josei Kaiho Renraku Kaigi Junbikai, "Erosu kaiho sengen" (Declaration of the liberation of Eros), August 1970, reprinted in Hist. JWL, 195.

20. Tanaka Mitsu for the Josei Kaiho Renraku Kaigi Junbikai, "Benjo kara no kaiho" (Liberation from being toilets), August 1970, reprinted in Hist. JWL, 202–3.

21. Group Tatakau Onna, "Haha e no rabu reta" (Love letter to Mother), May 1971, reprinted in Hist. JWL, 242–3.

22. Group Tatakau Onna, May 16, 1971, reprinted in Hist. JWL, 246.

23. Group Tatakau Onna, "Okasan e" (To Mother), August 1971, reprinted in Hist. JWL, 246.

24. Onna Sensen, Nov. 19, 1970, reprinted in Hist. JWL, 109.

25. Tanaka Mitsu for Josei Kaiho Renraku Kaigi Junbikai, "Erosu kaiho sengen" (Declaration of the liberation of Eros), August 1970, reprinted in Hist. JWL, 195.

26. Sakamoto Yoshie, "Kazoku kaitai o kokoromitsuzukete" (A continuing attempt to dismantle the family), *Shiso no kagaku* 102 (March 1979). The author later published an account of her experiences under the title *Kekkon yori mo ii kankei: Hikon no kazokuron* (A relationship even better than marriage: A nonmarital theory of the family) (Kyoto: Jinbun Shoin, 1988).

27. Ochiai Emiko, "Kindai to feminizumu" (The modern era and feminism), in Joseigaku Kenkyukai, ed., *Koza joseigaku 4: Onna no me de miru* (Women's studies series, vol. 4: Seeing with women's eyes) (Tokyo: Keiso Shobo, 1987). Reprinted in Ochiai, *Kindai kazoku to feminizumu* (The modern family and feminism) (Tokyo: Keiso Shobo, 1989), 214–39.

28. For Germany's case, see Himeoka Toshiko, *Kindai Doitsu no boseishugi feminizumu* (Maternalist feminism in modern Germany) (Tokyo: Keiso Shobo, 1993).

29. Jo Freeman, *The Politics of Women's Liberation* (New York: David McKay, 1975), 17–18.

30. Betty Friedan, *The Feminine Mystique* (New York: Norton, 1963).

31. See Ochiai, "Kindai to feminizumu" (see note 26), Chapter 9.

32. The critiques of the family developed in the early seventies by male intellectuals (among them Yoshimoto Takaaki and Okuma Nobuyuki) showed a similar failure to move beyond the ideal of the modern family.

7. The "New Family" Meets the Housewife's Malaise
1. Economic Planning Agency, *Kokumin seikatsu hakusho Showa 51 nendoban* (White paper on the national life for fiscal 1976) (Tokyo, 1976), 139.
2. "Sengokko fufu" (When postwar babies marry), *Asahi Shimbun*, February–July 1976. This newspaper series appeared under the following subheadings, between the dates indicated: "The dynamics of married couples," February 9–23, 1976; "The new family," March 15–25, 1976; "Childbirth and child rearing," April 20–29, 1976; "Two generations," June 21–July 1, 1976.
3. Ibid., "The new family."
4. Ibid., "The dynamics of married couples."
5. Prime Minister's Office, *Fujin ni kansuru ishiki chosa* (Opinion survey concerning women) (Tokyo, 1973).
6. "Saikin no fufu no ishiki chosa" (A survey of recent attitudes among married couples), *Asahi Shimbun*, February 2–3, 1976. The survey was conducted in Tokyo during January. The subjects were 206 married men and 274 married women living in a housing complex with many residents in the age group 20–39 years.
7. Ibid.
8. Ibid. See also "Nyu famiri no seikatsu repoto" (Report on the daily lives of new families), *Croissant*, July 1977. The latter survey was conducted in 1976 among young couples nationwide.
9. *Asahi Shimbun* survey (see note 6).
10. "Jitsu wa obake datta? Nyu famiri" (The new family: Was it really a phantom?) *Asahi Shimbun*, September 16, 1977.
11. Ibid. See also Yuzawa Yasuhiko, "Sosetsu" (General survey), *Kateika kyoiku*, special issue (March 1978).
12. Virtually all the existing studies of the "new family" as such have been cited above in the notes to this chapter. There are, however, numerous recent publications dealing with the attitudes of baby boomers after they ceased to be called "new families."
    These include: Editors of *Gekkan Akurosu*, ed., *Oinaru meiso: Dankai sedai samayoi no rekishi to genzai* (The great meandering: The baby-boom generation's wanderings, past and present) (Tokyo: Parco Shuppan, 1989); "Dankai sedai no ishiki chosa" (Attitude survey of the baby boom generation), *Akurosu*, August 1990; Prime Minister's Secretariat, Public Relations Office, *Sengo bebi bumu sedai no seikatsu ishiki* (Attitudes to daily life in the postwar baby-boom generation) (Tokyo, 1990); Hyogo-ken Katei Mondai Kenkyujo, *Dankai no sedai no seikatsu ishiki ni kansuru chosa kenkyu hokokusho: Josei no raifukosu o chushin ni* (Report of a study of attitudes to daily life in the baby-boom generation, centered on the life choices of women) (Kobe: Hyogo-ken Katei Mondai Kenkyujo, 1992); Kaizuka Yasunori, "JNN deta banku kara, no. 216: Dankai no sedai (shufu) wa junia no shiri o tataku no ga osuki" (From the Japan News Network data bank, no. 216: The baby boomer housewife likes to prod junior along), *Chosa joho*, October 1990.
13. For a survey of historical changes in the visual images of men and women in postwar Japanese women's magazines, see Ochiai Emiko, "Decent Housewives and Sensual White Women: Representations of Women of Postwar Japanese Magazines," *Japan Review* (International Research Center for Japanese Studies) 9 (1997): 151–169; Ochiai Emiko, "Bijuaru imeji toshite no onna" (Women as visual image), in Joseishi Sogo Kenkyukai, ed., *Nihon josei seikatsushi* (A history of the daily lives of Japanese women), vol. 5: *Gendai* (The present) (Tokyo: University of Tokyo Press, 1990), 203–34.
14. *Asahi Shimbun* survey (see note 6).
15. Ochiai, "Decent Housewives" (see note 13), 157.
16. Kyodo News Service, ed., *Nihonjin no sei* (Sexuality of the Japanese) (Tokyo: Bungei Shunju, 1984), 233–236.

17. Yuzawa Yasuhiko, "Nyu famiri kanken" (A personal view of the new family), *UP* no. 66, April 1978.

18. Quoted in "Sengokko fufu," *Asahi Shimbun*, March 15, 1976 (see note 2).

19. Nakano Osamu, "Arukihajimeta nyu famiri" (The new family has started walking), *Tsukuru*, September 1976.

20. Saito Shigeo, *Tsumatachi no shishuki* (The autumnal crisis of married women) (Tokyo: Kyodo News Service, 1982).

21. Ochiai, "Decent Housewives" (see note 13), 164.

22. Ochiai Emiko, *Kindai kazoku to feminizumu* (The modern family and feminism) (Tokyo: Keiso Shobo, 1989).

23. Takahashi Hisako, ed., *Kawariyuku fujin rodo* (Women's labor in transition) (Tokyo: Yuhikaku, 1983), Chapters 1 and 3.

24. Introduced in Hyogo-ken Katei Mondai Kenkyujo, *Dankai no sedai*, 29, 35 (see note 12).

25. Kyodo News Service, ed., *Nihonjin no sei* (see note 16), 233–236.

8.   Are Today's Parents Bad Parents?

1. Kyutoku Shigemori, *Bogenbyo* (Maternally induced diseases) (Tokyo: Kyoiku Kenkyusha, 1979; reprint, Tokyo: Sanmaku Shuppan, 1991), 185–6.

2. As mentioned in the Prologue, the indicators themselves could be said to have been constructed in such a way that they inevitably demonstrated the deterioration of the family. For example, the increase in the number of elderly people living alone (which is largely due to demographic factors) was included among the negative indices, and problems in the schools were also treated as domestic problems. Yuzawa Yasuhiko has frequently criticized the handling of family issues in the New Social Indicators (renamed the People's Life Indicators). For example, see Yuzawa Yasuhiko and Mori Mayumi, *Ima kazoku ni nayamu anata e* (To you who are worried about the family), (Tokyo: Companion Shuppan, 1985).

3. Ochiai Emiko, "Shinjinrui josei wa Agnes o mezasu ka?" (Will women of the new generation aim to be like Agnes?), *Fujin koron*, August 1988; reprinted in Ochiai, *Kindai kazoku to feminizumu* (The modern family and feminism) (Tokyo: Keiso Shobo, 1989), 280–94.

4. For mother-child interaction theory, see M. H. Klaus and J. H. Kennell, *Maternal-Infant Bonding* (Saint Louis: C. V. Mosby, 1976).

5. T. G. R. Bower, *A Primer of Infant Development* (San Francisco: W. H. Freeman, 1977); Ochiai Emiko, "Gendai no nyuyoji to sono oyatachi: Boshi kankei no shinwa to genjitsu" (Modern infants and their parents: Myths and realities of the mother-child relationship), in Ochiai Emiko, Misawa Kenichi et al., *Gendaijin no raifu kosu* (The life courses of contemporary people) (Kyoto: Minerva Shobo, 1989), 1–53.

6. Baba Kenichi and Kimura Sakae, *Boshi yuchaku* (Excessive closeness of mother and child) (Tokyo: Yuhikaku, 1988). In this unique study, one of the authors (Kimura) pursues the question of excessive closeness from the mother's viewpoint in great depth. Recently, modern theories of child rearing developed from the perspective of mothers, rather than doctors or educators, have at last begun to appear. For example, see also Hirao Keiko, *Kosodate sensen ijo ari* (All unquiet on the child-rearing front) (Tokyo: Chobunsha, 1992), and Yuki Misae, *Minna nayande mama ni naru* (All of us worry as we become mothers) (Tokyo: Chobunsha, 1990).

7. Makino Katsuko, "Nyuyoji o motsu hahaoya no seikatsu to 'ikuji fuan'" (The daily life and "child-rearing anxiety" of mothers with infant children), *Katei kyoiku kenkyusho kiyo* 3 (1982): 34–56.

8. Makino Katsuko, "Ikuji ni okeru 'fuan' ni tsuite" (On "anxiety" in child rearing), *Katei kyoiku kenkyusho kiyo* 2 (1981): 41–51; Makino Katsuko, "'Ikuji fuan' gainen to sono eikyo yoin ni tsuite no saikento" (A reexamination of the concept of "child-rearing anxiety" and the factors which influence it), loc. cit., no. 10 (1988): 23–31.

9. Hyogo-ken Katei Mondai Kenkyujo, *Kakukazoku no ikuji enjo ni kansuru chosa kenkyu hokokusho* (Report on a study concerning child-care support for nuclear families) (Kobe: Hyogo-ken Katei Mondai Kenkyujo, 1987). For a summary of this report, see Ochiai Emiko, "Ikuji enjo to ikuji nettowaku" (Child-care support and child-care networks), *Kazoku kenkyu* 1 (1989), reprinted in Ochiai, *Kindai kazoku to feminizumu*, 93–135 (see note 3).

10. Makino, "'Ikuji fuan' gainen" (see note 8), 30.

11. Makino Katsuko, "Nyuyoji o motsu hahaoya no gakushu katsudo e no sanka to ikuji fuan" (Participation of mothers with infants in learning activities, and its relation to child-rearing anxiety), *Katei kyoiku kenkyusho kiyo* 9 (1987).

12. Makino, "Nyuyoji o motsu hahaoya no seikatsu" (see note 7).

13. Hyogo-ken Katei Mondai Kenkyujo, *Kakukazoku no ikuji enjo* (see note 9), 22.

14. Yazawa Sumiko, "Gendai josei no kyo to ashita" (The present and future of modern women), in Office of Planning and Coordination for Women, Civic Affairs Bureau, Yokohama City Government, *Yokohama shimin josei no seikatsu jittai to ishiki chosa* (A survey of daily life and attitudes among women in Yokohama), part 2 (Yokohama, 1988).

15. Hyogo-ken Katei Mondai Kenkyujo, *Kakukazoku no ikuji enjo* (see note 9), 18.

16. Ibid., 115–125.

17. Ibid., 14–15.

18. Philippe Ariès, "The Family and the City," *Daedalus* 106, no. 2 (1977): 235.

9. Bilaterality and the Future of the *Ie*

1. Hiroshima Kiyoshi, "Jakunen yuhaigu danshi no setai keisei doko: Kako to mirai" (Trends in household formation by young married men: Past and future), *Jinkogaku kenkyu* 16 (1993): 1–15. Hiroshima ascribes the pre-1985 increase and the post-1985 decrease to a synthesis of two trends in opposite directions. "Until 1985, the ratio of potential co-residents increased rapidly due to the decline in the birthrate (and hence in the number of siblings) that had accompanied the demographic transition; as a result, the rate of co-residence increased. Between 1985 and 1990, however, the ratio of potential co-residents, then mainly in their twenties, essentially reached its upper limit of 90 percent; as a result, the decline in the ratio of actual to potential co-residence which had continued throughout this period can be said to have been directly expressed as a decline of the rate of co-residence." (The rate of co-residence is the product of the the the ratio of potential co-residents and the ratio of actual to potential co-residence.)

2. Ochiai Emiko, "Terebi no kazokutachi wa doshite kagayaku no ka" (Why are television's families radiant?), in *Bessatsu takarajima 110: 80-nendai no shotai* (Takarajima special issue 110: The true nature of the 80s) (Tokyo: JICC, 1990).

3. This problem is also pointed out in Tsubouchi Reiko, *Nihon no kazoku* (The family in Japan) (Kyoto: Academia, 1992), 2–3.

4. For a discussion which focuses on this point, see Kurosu Satomi and Ochiai Emiko, "Adoption as an Heirship Strategy under Demographic Constraints: A Case from Nineteenth-Century Japan," *Journal of Family History* 20, no. 3 (1995): 261–288.

5. The study by Kurosu and Ochiai, which investigated records for 33 villages in Tama in 1870, obtained the figure 20 percent.

6. Harafuji Hiroshi, in *Sozokuho no tokushitsu* (Special features of the law of succession) (Tokyo: Sobunsha, 1982), gives a figure of 39.7 percent for the Kanazawa domain in the late Edo Period.

7. Yuzawa Yasuhiko, "Nihon ni okeru muko yoshi engumi no tokeiteki taisei" (Statistical trends of son-in-law adoptions in Japan), *Atarashii kazoku* 30 (1983): 21–29.

8. Ibid.

9. Tsubouchi Yoshihiro and Maeda Narifumi, *Kakukazoku saiko* (The nuclear family reconsidered) (Tokyo: Kobundo, 1977); Kuchiba Masuo, Tsubouchi Yoshihiro, and

The LTCB International Library Foundation
Statement of Purpose

The world is moving steadily toward a borderless economy and deepening international interdependence. Amid this globalization of economic activities, the Japanese economy is developing organic ties with the economies of individual nations throughout the world via trade, direct investment, overseas manufacturing activities, and the international movement of capital.

As a result, interest in Japan's politics, economy, and society and in the concepts and values that lie behind Japan's socioeconomic activities is growing in many countries.

However, the overseas introduction and dissemination of translations of works originally written in Japanese lags behind the growth of interest in Japan. Such works are not well known outside Japan. One main reason for this is that the high costs involved in translating and publishing materials written in Japanese hinder the undertaking of such activities on a commercial basis. It is extremely important to overcome this barrier to deepen and broaden mutual understanding.

The LTCB International Library Foundation has been founded to address this pressing need. Its primary activity is to disseminate information on Japan in foreign countries through the translation of selected Japanese works on Japan's politics, economy, society, and culture into English and other languages and the publication and distribution of these translations. To commemorate the completion of The Long-Term Credit Bank of Japan, Ltd.'s new headquarters and its 40th anniversary, LTCB has provided the LTCB International Library Foundation with an endowment.

We sincerely hope that the LTCB International Library Foundation will successfully fulfill its mission of promoting global understanding and goodwill through enhanced cultural exchange.

March 1, 1994
The founders of the LTCB International Library Foundation